Olatunde Olanrewaju

The
Truth about
Rapture

The Truth About Rapture
ISBN 979-8-9875157-1-6
Copyright © 2022

You can contact us at:

therockfoundationmin@gmail.com
oladatunde@yahoo.co.uk

Cover and Book design by Hotprints Media
+1 7183005410 Email:artistkehindedada@gmail.com

Contents

Introduction

Matters concerning the end time, rapture, and the end of our world, as we know it, have been extensively talked about by many. Many doctrines about the end time and the time the rapture will take place have been taught and written in books by many, over the years. Many preachers have taken different positions on the matter. It is a topic of contention in the body of Christ. Surely, there is no confusion with God, for God is not the author of confusion as the Bible puts it in 1 Corinthians 14:33:

> *33. For God is not the author of confusion, but of peace, as in all churches of the saints.*

Therefore, I strongly believe that the Bible has a definite position on this matter, and it is not heaven's intention to hide the truth or to confuse us about the truth. I believe that the position of the Bible concerning the timing of rapture is plain and without ambiguity. And that if we give due diligence to the matter without any prejudice, we can clearly see the position of heaven concerning the timing of rapture in the pages of the Scriptures.

What we are particular about in this book is to know the position of the Bible with regard to the time rapture will occur. Rapture is a major event in Christendom. The early church members (the first generation of Christians) lived their lives in such a way that showed to the world around them that the second coming of Christ was imminent. It was in this reality they lived, moved, and had their being. They taught it to their followers at the slightest opportunity. For example, Paul went to Thessalonica and stayed there for three weeks. Within those three weeks, he had hundreds of brand-new believers. Paul, within those same three weeks, taught these brand-new believers about the second coming of our Lord and eternal judgment—the antichrist, rapture, you name it. Look at it in Act 17:1–3:

> *1. Now when they had passed through Amphipolis and Apollonia, they came to Thessalonica, where was a synagogue of the Jews: 2. And Paul, as his manner was, went in unto them, and three sabbath days reasoned with them out of the Scriptures, 3. Opening and alleging, that Christ must needs have suffered, and risen again from the dead; and that this Jesus, whom I preach unto you, is Christ.*

Paul and his team left Thessalonica after those three weeks of intense teaching and continued unto other places. After some time, a dispute about the matters of rapture and the end time arose in the church of Thessalonica, where Paul had spent three weeks teaching. Some preachers or prophets came by from other places to tell them that Christ had already come, and rapture had taken place. The church was thrown into confusion by this teaching. The elders of the church, knowing where Paul was at that time, decided to send messengers to Paul for clarification of the issue. The response of Paul was what gave birth to the second book Paul wrote to the Thessalonians. We shall talk more about the book and the dispute later on in this book. But what I am trying to bring to your attention here is that the matter of rapture is so important that it is part of the foundational class for new believers. Paul thought it the right thing to do when he took great time and efforts to educate a three-week-old group of believers about all they needed to know about the matters of the end time, eternal judgement, the antichrist, and rapture. Look at Hebrews 6:1–2:

> *1.   Therefore leaving the principles of the doctrine of Christ, let us go on unto perfection; not laying again the foundation of repentance from dead works, and of faith toward God, 2. Of the doctrine of baptisms, and of laying on of hands, and **of resurrection of the dead, and of eternal judgment.***

Notice what the Bible calls the foundation class of Christianity. Look at the last two items in the list. Resurrection from the dead, which is what happens when rapture takes place, and eternal judgement, which also covers everything around the matter of the antichrist and the end of time.

Now then, right from the inception, the devil has been doing everything possible to get the body of Christ confused about this so-called fundamental topic of Christianity, just like we see in the church

4

of Thessalonica. The deception started in the days of the founding fathers of Christianity. Hence, this issue we are addressing today is as old as Christianity itself.

My desire is that as the body of Christ read this book; it will lead us to a personal search through the Scriptures, just like the Berean Christians, to see what the Bible says concerning the timing of rapture. In this book, I have highlighted certain Scriptures that will lead us to the truth of the timing of rapture. But most importantly, the reader, through the help of the Holy Spirit, should look at the passages mentioned in the book and see if these things be true. Beyond that, I also hope that the reader will do a personal search through the pages of the Scripture to see if these things be true.

Christianity is a walk with God. No one knows the way to the Father except Jesus. Jesus clearly tells us about this in John 14:5–6:

> *5. Thomas saith unto him, Lord, we know not whither thou goest; and how can we know the way? 6. Jesus saith unto him, I am the way, the truth, and the life:* ***no man cometh unto the Father, but by me***

Notice that the disciple, Thomas, asks the question on our behalf; where is the way to the Father? How can we know You more? How can we live the Christian life? How can we walk with God? These and many more questions along this line are frequently asked questions in our Christian journey. Our Lord Jesus has graciously answered that question even before we came to Him. He is the way to the Father. You want to walk with God? Go through the Son. Jesus, who is the Word (John 1:1), gave us Himself in order to easily navigate our way through this Christian Journey. Look at how the psalmist puts it in Psalm 119:105:

> *105. Thy word is a lamp unto my feet, and a light unto my path.*

Did you see how He frames it? God's word is a lamp unto my feet. What does that mean? It means in a very dark world, I need a torch light to be able to navigate my way through the dark so as not to stumble and fall. With the torch light, I can safely take my steps in life

6

without falling or failing. Look at the second part of the passage. The word is also a light unto my path. This is a bigger picture compared to the first. In the first part, he talks about my daily steps. But in the second part, he is talking about a bigger picture. My path in life. The path I am expected to follow. My course (2 Timothy 4:7), ministry, career goals and aspirations, marriage, relationship with people, bringing up children, you name it. The light of God, which indeed is the Word of God, can help navigate us through all these paths in life. Therefore, just like Google map or GPS, the word of God has a voice through which He can tell us the steps to take and the path to take. Now then, the Word and the light is one just as John puts it in John 1:1–5:

> *1. In the beginning was the Word, and the Word was with God, and the Word was God. 2. The same was in the beginning with God. 3. All things were made by him; and without him was not any thing made that was made. 4. In him was life; and the life was the light of men. 5. And the light shineth in darkness; and the darkness comprehended it not.*

Can you see how it is put in the passages above? First the Word was in the beginning and that same Word is God. The same Word who is God became the light of men. Hence, the Word is the same as the light. Therefore, you cannot get to God unless you go through Jesus. Jesus is the Word and the Light through which you can get to the Father. In view of this, we can confidently say that the Word is a very important part of our walk with God. That means it must be simple and clear enough in other not to misdirect or mislead us when we are trying to navigate our way through to the heart of the Father.

Now then, the Bible has a voice and it does speak. By this we mean, it takes a specific stand/position on every matter that concerns humans. By this voice we can navigate our way through life without stumbling or falling. However, just like some drivers, at times, choose to ignore the voice of the GPS and go in their own direction, believers also sometimes silence the voice of the Bible and make it go in the direction they want it to go (or better still, they silence the voice of the Bible and make the Bible say what they want to hear. As believers, that is a very dangerous thing to do. Look at how a wise man puts it in Proverbs 16:25:

> *25. There is a way that seemeth right unto a man, but the end thereof are the ways of death.*

The end is always destruction. This world is a dark place. We can only successfully navigate our way through it by giving preeminence to the Word of God and allowing it to lead us, whether it is convenient or not, whether it is comfortable or not, whether it is what we want to hear or not. That is the ONLY way to enjoy a walk with God and make it to eternity with God. Look at how the Holy Ghost, through Peter, puts it in Acts 4:12:

8

12. Neither is there salvation in any other: for there is none other name under heaven given among men, whereby we must be saved.

Salvation in that passage is not necessarily restricted to the initial being saved from bondage of sin and Satan. We all need continuous salvation. Our walk with God is a progressive walk. Each step higher is a salvation from the previous step. And we cannot go to the next step by our own idea; it has to be by the Word of God, which is a lamp unto our feet and a light unto our path. If we have to put these four passages together (John 14:5–6, Psalm 119:105, Proverbs 16:25 and Act 4:12), we can clearly and safely conclude that the Bible has a voice, and the voice directs our path. It is dangerous to make the Bible say what suits you or make it say what it is not saying. Yes, anyone can pick any portion of the Bible and make it say whatever he/she wants it to say. That, my friends, is a dangerous thing to do and can lead to destruction. That is why God has put some safety measures in place in order to prevent us from unknowingly doing that. Look at one of the safety measures in 2 Corinthians 13:1:

1. This is the third time I am coming to you. In the mouth of two or three witnesses shall every word be established.

Did you notice the words "shall every word be established"? What could that mean? It means that a word or a matter can only gain establishment or can only stand if it can be collaborated by two or three witnesses. It means that it is not safe to build any doctrine on one passage. No thought or idea should become a doctrine if it is standing on only one passage. There has to be at least two passages to collaborate or support the doctrine.

This reminds me of the story of a young man who desperately wanted to hear from God. However, every attempt of his to hear God failed. Finally, he decided to make God speak to him through the Bible. So, he said a short prayer: "Dear Lord, please let it be that whatever passage I open will be the word you want to speak to me." He opened the Bible and his finger fell on Matthew 27:5, which says:

> *5. And he cast down the pieces of silver in the temple, and departed, and went and hanged himself.*

He read it and didn't quite understand what God was saying. So, he prayed again, "Lord, I am going to open the Bible again. Speak to me through your word." He again opened the Scripture and his finger fell on Luke 10:37, which says:

> *37. And he said, He that shewed mercy on him. Then said Jesus unto him, Go, and do thou likewise.*

Hence, he concluded that God was asking him to commit suicide, just like Judas did, because the passage his finger fell on the second time says go and do likewise. Now, consider the case of this young man. We know that God speaks to His children through the Scriptures, but we also know that that is not the way to hear God's voice through the Scriptures. That is more or less making, or better still, forcing the Bible to say what you want to hear or what you want it to say. In order to really make the Bible speak for itself rather than we insinuating, we have to look at verses through the eye of the context.

Another danger we sometimes find ourselves in, as per interpreting and teaching the word, is the danger of giving the wrong interpretation to passages. Paul puts it this way in 2 Timothy 2:15:

> *15. Study to shew thyself approved unto God, a workman that needeth not to be ashamed, **rightly dividing the word of truth**.*

Did you notice the last statement in that verse? "Rightly dividing the word of truth." That means that we can either rightly divide the word or wrongly divide the word. What does divide mean? The word divide means to teach the truth directly and correctly. If there is no possibility of wrongly teaching the word, Paul will not mention it. Let me show you another passage to show that it is possible for genuine and sincere Christians to wrongly divide the word. Let's look at 2 Peter 3:14–16:

11

14. Wherefore, beloved, seeing that ye look for such things, be diligent that ye may be found of him in peace, without spot, and blameless. 15. And account that the longsuffering of our Lord is salvation; even as our beloved brother Paul also according to the wisdom given unto him hath written unto you; 16. As also in all his epistles, speaking in them of these things; in which are some things hard to be understood, which they that are unlearned and unstable wrest, as they do also the other Scriptures, unto their own destruction.

Notice that this is another author affirming that the word can be wrongly taught. In the first passage we considered, Paul is admonishing his disciple, Timothy, to study very hard in other not to teach the wrong things to the congregation. Here, Peter, another follower of Christ, is also teaching his congregation that some believers have taken the teachings of Paul and other Scriptures and have taught it wrongly, and that this act has led to their destruction. Hence, from the above two passages, we can gather that even though the Bible has a right meaning to every passage, genuine and sincere believers can get a wrong interpretation from it and also teach this to their followers. This also can be a dangerous act and can lead to the destruction of many.

With these thoughts at the back of our mind, let us consider the matter at hand—the timing of the rapture.

Chapter 2

The Contention

There are three major schools of thought with regard to rapture: Pre-tribulation rapture (The rapture taking place just before the antichrist is revealed and before the great tribulation starts); Mid-tribulation rapture (the rapture taking place after the antichrist is revealed and at the midpoint of the seven-year reign of the antichrist, just before the great tribulation); and Post-tribulation rapture (the rapture happening at the end of the seven-year reign of the antichrist, just after the great tribulation and before the day of the Lord). It will be misleading if the Bible has these three doctrines. God can never mislead His children. It will also be unfair if the Bible is not clear about its position on the timing of such an important matter, for how can we navigate our way through this time if the lamp for our feet is dim? Or else, how can the light to our path go dim at the most important time in the history of humanity? Look at what Paul says concerning such matters in 1 Corinthians 14:8:

> *8. For if the trumpet give an uncertain sound, who shall prepare himself to the battle?*

The human army and watchmen do not give uncertain sound when they need to inform the people about what is to come. Why should the Almighty God, who loves us well enough to give us His only Son, do such a thing?

The vast majority of Christians stand with the pre-tribulation and the mid-tribulation schools of thought (the pre-tribulation seems more popular). The debate between these two can get heated at times, and no one wants to back down for the other. We all want our voices to be louder than that of our neighbor's while we completely silence or ignore the voice of the Bible on the issue. Each seems to have strong reasons to support why their position about the rapture is the truth. Definitely, rapture cannot occur thrice, and so one of the three has to be accurate. It might also be that none of the three is correct. What will be most appropriate for us to do is to take a step back, lay down our position, prejudices, and arms and pay attention to what the Bible has to say on the matter. The only way to do that is to come with an open mind, an empty cup if you will, so that God can fill it with His truth

It is important to pay attention to the position of the "author and finisher" of the matter. Fortunately for us, God has not left us in darkness concerning His position as to when the rapture will occur. He has meticulously planted everything we should know about when the rapture will be in the most accessible book in the universe–the Bible.

The purpose of this book is to prove beyond all reasonable doubt, from the most authentic source–the Bible–the position of God concerning the timing of rapture. We shall together examine Scripture after Scripture to see what God has to say about the timing, as that is more important than what any Bishop or general overseer or professor of eschatology would have to say. In order to put things in better perspective, let us define some common terms used in the matter of the end that has been affecting our understanding of the timing.

Definition of terms

One of the areas that brings confusion in the matter of the end time is the definition of terms. A clear biblical definition of the related terms used in the matter of the end time will help us put a lot of things in perspective.

Rapture

Rapture is a phenomenon or event, if you like, that most (if not all) believers in Christ are looking forward to. Interestingly, the word "rapture" is not written anywhere in the Bible. It was actually coined from the words "caught up" as seen in 1 Thessalonians 4:16–18:

> *16. For the Lord himself shall descend from heaven with a shout, with the voice of the archangel, and with the trump of God: and the dead in Christ shall rise first: 17. Then we which are alive and remain shall be caught up together with them in the clouds, to meet the Lord in the air: and so shall we ever be with the Lord. 18. Wherefore comfort one another with these words.*

15

The two words, caught up, are from a Greek word (harpadzo), which means to seize or carry off by force. When translated to Latin, it means rapio. The word "rapture" is taken from the Latin (rapio) of the two words (caught up).

Hence, even though the word rapture is not written anywhere in the Bible, the majority of Christians would agree that the phenomenon is explained in many parts of the Bible. Let us do a quick summary of the event based on descriptions we can see from the Bible.

According to the Scriptures, the phenomenon called rapture will happen suddenly, when no one expects it. Christians who are alive will be forcefully caught up into the sky at the sound of the trumpet of God and a loud voice of an archangel. A lot of movies have depicted people leaving their clothing behind during this occurrence. The Bible didn't say any such thing. But that doesn't matter much anyway. What matters is that the Christians who are alive then will be in the sky with Jesus. That is exactly how the above passage (1 Thessalonians 4:16–18) described it. Another fact to note about rapture is that those Christians who died in Christ before that time will suddenly come back to life. That probably means graves will pop open all over the world. This will actually occur first, before the Christians who are alive will join them. Now then, another aspect not mentioned in the above passage is the issue of we being changed. Look at how Paul puts it in 1 Corinthians 15:52–53:

16

52. In a moment, in the twinkling of an eye, at the last trump: for the trumpet shall sound, and the dead shall be raised incorruptible, and we shall be changed. 53. For this corruptible must put on incorruption, and this mortal must put on immortality.

If you notice, the passage gives an idea of the kind of change that will take place. This corruptible body will become incorruptible, and this mortal body will become immortal. The details of this are beyond the scope of this book, so we shall not talk about it. Many other passages give us one or two more hint about rapture, but let's stick to these two. We shall look at other details in a later section of this book.

Now then, the majority in the body of Christ will agree with the above description of rapture. Notice that we didn't say anything that the Bible didn't say. A good number of Christians believe that it is an event that will happen someday, and many are looking forward to it. The only thing most Christians don't agree on is when it will happen.

Wrath of God

In the King James Version (KJV) of the Bible, the word "Wrath" is mentioned 198 times both in the New and Old Testament. Most of it has nothing to do with the end time, even though it carries the same meaning. We shall consider a few that relate to the matters of the end for better understanding. The common passage used by many to support their position regarding the timing of rapture is in 1 Thessalonians 5:9:

> *9. For God hath not appointed us to wrath, but to obtain salvation by our Lord Jesus Christ,*

The word wrath in that passage is from a Greek word (orge), which means anger, punishment, indignation, vengeance, or any violent emotion, especially anger. It also means any kind of punishment inflicted by magistrates. Therefore, we can see that the passage is actually talking to Christians (if you read from the beginning so as not to take it out of context). Looking at the same passage from verse one, it should be noted that Paul is talking to the church in Thessalonica about "the day of the Lord." That's not rapture. Take a look at it here 1 Thessalonians 5:1–3:

> *1. But of the times and the seasons, brethren, ye have no need that I write unto you. 2. For yourselves know perfectly that the **day of the Lord** so cometh as a thief in the night. 3. For when they shall say, Peace and safety; then sudden destruction cometh upon them, as travail upon a woman with child; and they shall not escape.*

18

Did you notice he is talking about the day of the Lord and not rapture? Did you also notice that the day of the Lord is the day of reckoning for the unbelievers? Hence, when he says in Verse 9 above that we are not appointed unto wrath, he is saying that we are not going to be part of those that will experience God's judgment on the day of the Lord. Why? Let's look at another passage, for we cannot build a doctrine on a single passage. Isaiah 13:9–13:

> *9. Behold, the day of the LORD cometh, cruel both with wrath and fierce anger, to lay the land desolate: and he shall destroy the sinners thereof out of it. 10. For the stars of heaven and the constellations thereof shall not give their light: the sun shall be darkened in his going forth, and the moon shall not cause her light to shine. 11. And I will punish the world for their evil, and the wicked for their iniquity; and I will cause the arrogancy of the proud to cease, and will lay low the haughtiness of the terrible. 12. I will make a man more precious than fine gold; even a man than the golden wedge of Ophir. 13. Therefore, I will shake the heavens, and the earth shall remove out of her place, in the wrath of the LORD of hosts, and in the day of his fierce anger.*

It's a long read, but it's worth it. This passage fully describes the wrath of God on the day of the Lord. And we can see clearly from the passage that the wrath of God will only be poured out on the world for their evil and their sin. Hence, it is clear from the above two passages that Christians are not appointed unto the wrath of God because we have believed in the Son of God. And it is also clear that the wrath of God is completely different from tribulation. Another word for wrath is God's judgment. This is mostly used in the Old Testament. However, some passages in the New Testament also refer to God's wrath as God's judgment, like Romans 1:32:

> *32. Who knowing the judgment of God, that they which commit such things are worthy of death, not only do the same, but have pleasure in them that do them.*

In the above passage, Paul is talking about the judgment of God falling on the unbelievers who refuse to repent. Other passages that talk about God pouring out His wrath on the unbelievers include Zephaniah 1: 14–18, Joel 1: 15, and 2 Peter 3:10, just to mention but a few. You can check them out for more clarification. The wrath of God, simply put, is the judgment of God unleashed on unrepentant sinners after several attempts at getting them to repent have failed.

Tribulation

The word tribulation means persecution, intense pressure,

20

affliction, or oppression. The word tribulation appears twenty-two times in the KJV Bible, and the word tribulations appears four times in the KJV Bible. Out of the twenty-six times tribulation(s) appears in the Bible, only twice is it used in relation to the unbelievers. The rest (twenty-four) times, it is used in relation to believers. It is used when Christians are to be tried, refined, or made better. The majority of believers will agree that persecution only applies to believers—generally speaking, it's the difficulties the devil throws at believers to get them offtrack. Look at this passage: Matthew 13:20–21:

> *20. But he that received the seed into stony places, the same is he that heareth the word, and anon with joy receiveth it; 21. Yet hath he not root in himself, but dureth for a while: for when tribulation or persecution ariseth because of the word, by and by he is offended.*

Notice that in that passage, tribulation is a tool used by the devil to pull believers down from their track. And notice that it only arises in the life of the believer because of the word he's received. On the other hand, it is used as a stepping stone by God to build the spiritual strength and stamina of believers. Let's look at how Peter puts it in 1 Peter 4:12–13:

> *12. Beloved, think it not strange concerning the fiery*

21

trial which is to try you, as though some strange thing happened unto you: 13. But rejoice, inasmuch as ye are partakers of Christ's sufferings; that, when his glory shall be revealed, ye may be glad also with exceeding joy.

All through the life of a believer, he/she must expect to have persecution (tribulation). Notice what Peter says in the above passage. It should not be strange to us when we go through trials (tribulation). It should be a thing of joy because at the end of it, we shall be rewarded. Our Lord Jesus took His time to prepare us for this. Take a look at what He says shortly before He leaves the earth: John 16:33:

33. These things I have spoken unto you, that in me ye might have peace. In the world ye shall have tribulation: but be of good cheer; I have overcome the world.

Did you notice that Jesus doesn't say we *might* have tribulation? He says we *shall*. Nothing can change it. It is part of our Christian journey. Saying we can avoid tribulation is just like saying a man can become a professor in a specialty without passing any exam. That's impossible. We cannot run away from tribulation and we cannot avoid it. Take a look at how Paul puts it in Act 14:22:

22. Confirming the souls of the disciples, and exhorting them to continue in the faith, and that we must through much tribulation enter into the kingdom of God.

Did you notice what Paul says in the passage above? We must through much tribulation enter into the kingdom of God. It is inevitable. You cannot be a believer and not go through tribulation. Now let's consider one passage along this line that speaks specifically about end time. Look at it in Revelation 7:13–14:

> *13. And one of the elders answered, saying unto me, What are these which are arrayed in white robes? and whence came they? 14. And I said unto him, Sir, thou knowest. And he said to me, These are they which came out of great tribulation, and have washed their robes, and made them white in the blood of the Lamb.*

Notice that this passage is not just talking about tribulation, it is talking about great tribulation. And notice that the people it talks of that have undergone it are not unbelievers. They are believers who have been purified as gold is purified by passing through fire. Take a look at another passage in 1 Thessalonians. The same letter in which Paul tells the Thessalonians that believers are not subject to God's wrath; 1 Thessalonians 3:4:

> *4. For verily, when we were with you, we told you before that we should suffer tribulation; even as it came to pass, and ye know.*

23

Can you see how it is clearly stated in this passage that believers must suffer tribulation? To give a summary, tribulation is applicable to the believers, while wrath is for the unbelievers. Tribulation is not from God, like we saw earlier on. It is the devil's attempt to make us deny Jesus. Wrath is from God, and it is to punish the unbelievers for not repenting and refusing to accept the finished work of Christ. Tribulation is never meant to destroy believers; rather, it is meant to purify them and make them better, just as gold is refined by passing it through fire. The wrath of God is meant to completely destroy the root cause of sin. Sometimes, if not most times, it involves the complete destruction of the unrepentant sinners. There usually are several warnings before God unleashes His wrath, but there are no warnings before tribulation. Yes, sometimes, you get a heads-up of the coming tribulation, but the heads-up is not to help you escape it; it is usually to prepare your mind to be able to go through it.

The day of the Lord

The day of the Lord is a day in which God will pour His wrath upon the nations that have refused to repent for their deeds. This day is the day that the wrath we discussed earlier will be poured out. There are eighty-six verses of the Bible that speak about this day. All of them look at the day from various angles, though there are other parts of the Bible that describe the event of that day without calling it the day of the Lord. Let's discuss a few and see what the day is about.

24

Let's start with Zephaniah 1:14–18:

> *14. The great **day of the LORD** is near, it is near, and hasteth greatly, even the voice of the day of the LORD: the mighty man shall cry there bitterly. 15. That day is a day of wrath, a day of trouble and distress, a day of wasteness and desolation, a day of darkness and gloominess, a day of clouds and thick darkness, 16. A day of the trumpet and alarm against the fenced cities, and against the high towers. 17. And I will bring distress upon men, that they shall walk like blind men, because they have sinned against the LORD: and their blood shall be poured out as dust, and their flesh as the dung. 18. Neither their silver nor their gold shall be able to deliver them in the day of the LORD's wrath; but the whole land shall be devoured by the fire of his jealousy: for he shall make even a speedy riddance of all them that dwell in the land.*

From the passage above, we can see that the day of the Lord is nearby. We can also see that it is the day when God will pour out His wrath on the earth. Notice that this wrath will be poured out only on those who have sinned against God and refused to repent. Hence, this is in line with the passages we considered earlier about the description of God's wrath. We can also see that the day will bring great distress upon all men everywhere on earth. There shall be no place of escape.

Let us consider another passage. Joel 1:15:

> *15. Alas for the day!* **for the day of the LORD** *is at hand, and as a destruction from the Almighty shall it come.*

There we see again that the day of the Lord brings destruction. Even though this passage does not mention who this destruction is for, we know from the two previous passages that it is for those who do not fear the Lord. And again, we can see that it clearly states that the destruction is from God. Let us look at one more example from the New Testament: 2 Peter 3:10:

> *10. But the* **day of the Lord** *will come as a thief in the night; in the which the heavens shall pass away with a great noise, and the elements shall melt with fervent heat, the earth also and the works that are therein shall be burned up.*

This New Testament passage is also saying the same thing that the passages in the Old Testament are saying. It is the day God will pour out His wrath upon the wicked. Putting everything together, the day of the Lord is the day that God will pour His wrath upon the earth. Hence, we can see the relationship between the day of the Lord and the Wrath of God. You will also notice, in the above passage, that the day of the Lord will come as a thief in the night. What this means is that it will come suddenly, at a time the unbelievers are not

26

expecting it. Let me show you two passages to prove that: 2 Peter 3:10:

> *10. But the **day of the Lord will come as a thief** in the night; in the which the heavens shall pass away with a great noise, and the elements shall melt with fervent heat, the earth also and the works that are therein shall be burned up.*

Did you notice the phrase "as a thief in the night"? Let's look at another passage, for out of the mouth of two or three witnesses, every word shall be established: 1 Thessalonians 5:1–3

> *1. But of the times and the seasons, brethren, ye have no need that I write unto you. 2. For yourselves know perfectly that the day of the Lord so cometh as a thief in the night. 3. For when they shall say, Peace and safety; then sudden destruction cometh upon them, as travail upon a woman with child; and they shall not escape.*

There goes the phrase again. Notice that each time the phrase is used, it is used in relation to the unbelievers. This suggest to us that the preachers, in both cases, are trying to communicate to their audience (which includes us) that the wrath of God is an event that will happen when the unbelievers least expect it. Now let's do a recap.

The wrath of God is an event that will occur at the end of time, and it is not for believers. It is for the unbelievers. And the wrath will come upon them suddenly because they are in darkness. The wrath of God will come upon the earth on a day referred to as the day of the Lord (you will also see that phrase in all the above passages and many others).

The second coming

Just like rapture, the phrase, "the second coming" is not written in the Bible. The second coming is a phrase coined by believers to describe Christ's promise to us that He is coming back again. However, the second coming is described with phrases like: His appearing, the coming of our Lord, the coming of the Son of Man, when He appears, the day of Christ, etc. Almost every book of the New Testament talked about the second coming either directly or indirectly. If we were to review all the passages in the New Testament that say something about the second coming of our Lord, this book might run out of space. However, for the purpose of understanding, let's review a few of the passages so that we can have an idea of what the day is about. Hebrews 9:28:

> *28. So Christ was once offered to bear the sins of many; and unto them that look for him shall he appear the second time without sin unto salvation.*

28

Looking at this passage closely, we can clearly see that it tells of the first and the second coming of Christ. In the first coming, He came as the Lamb who took away the sin of any who would dare to believe in Him. He is coming back to give us the ultimate salvation, not from sin, but from mortality and corruption, which is the ultimate salvation. Let's look at another passage: Titus 2:13–14:

> *13. Looking for that blessed hope, and the glorious appearing of the great God and our Saviour Jesus Christ; 14. Who gave himself for us, that he might redeem us from all iniquity, and purify unto himself a peculiar people, zealous of good works.*

Here we see the phrase glorious appearing, which is another phrase used to described the second coming of our Lord. We also see in the same passage that it is a blessed hope that all believers should look forward to. Hence, it is a core doctrine in Christendom, and efforts must be made to know as much as possible concerning what the Bible has to say about it. Even Jesus talked about His second coming in many passages in the Gospels. Take a look at one of them: Mathew 16:27–28:

> *27. For the Son of man shall come in the glory of his Father with his angels; and then he shall reward every man according to his works. 28. Verily I say unto you, There be some standing here, which shall*

29

not taste of death, till they see the Son of man coming in his kingdom.

Here, the Lord is telling of His second coming. Again, we see here that Christ is coming to reward and to judge and not to die for sins again. That is the more reason why believers should look forward to it. Let's look at one more passage before we wrap this up. Reward usually comes after judgement, as it is mentioned in 2 Timothy 4:1:

> *1. I charge thee therefore before God, and the Lord Jesus Christ, who shall judge the quick and the dead at his appearing and his kingdom;*

Here, we see the phrase "at His appearing" used to describe the second coming. We can also see that when He comes, He will judge both the living and the dead. Putting everything together, the second coming is a phrase that is not written anywhere in the Bible, but other phrases used to describe the event are used. The second coming is the event that will lead to rapture, or better put, it is the event that will usher in the rapture or an event that will immediately precede the rapture. Therefore, we can say that the Wrath of God and the day of the Lord go together and they are intended for the unbelievers, while the rapture and the coming of our Lord Jesus Christ go together and are intended for the believers. There are some that say the second coming and rapture are events that are seven years apart. We have not seen this belief reflected in the passages we have considered so far, but we shall look at the two (rapture and the second coming) events in more details in the latter part of this book.

Why should we bother about the Timing?

At the moment, the church has no unified position on the timing of rapture. Due to the extensive argument around this topic, many Christians have taken a very dangerous position about it: "Whenever the rapture happens, I will make it." This statement cannot be farther from the truth than any other statement. It is the enemy's trick to prevent us from getting God's best.

Each doctrine concerning the timing of rapture requires different levels of preparation. For the pre- and mid-tribulation rapture doctrines, all the believer needs to do is just remain faithful as a Christian and live a good Christian life. There is nothing to lose here. We continue our jobs and live in our houses until rapture comes. But for the post-tribulation rapture believers, a different level of preparation is required. In addition to a life that pleases God, the believer has to learn patience and resistance to oppression and be ready to stand even when it is difficult to do so. The believer has to be ready to lose his/her job, house, and access to the basic amenities of life (to mention but a few) if he/she must reject the mark. Take a look at the test run God gave us during the pandemic. How well did we do? The majority of us fell like a pack of cards. Zero preparation, zero endurance. Do you think that with the current level of preparation, we will be able to stand in the face of the greatest persecution in human history? Unfortunately, in this generation we have not seen much of the kind of persecution the early Christians saw. Although in some parts of the world Christians have suffered persecution even unto death, the majority of Christians in this generation have undergone much of the same. Now we are talking about the great tribulation, which has no precedence in human history. What this means is that what happened to the disciples of the early church is child's play compared to what we shall experience. Hence, if the post-tribulation rapture doctrine is true, then we are in grave danger because practically no church is teaching us how to survive what is coming. Now you can see that taking the wrong position as per the timing of rapture is an extremely dangerous fit.

I remember the story of that young man who had a marathon race. The entire distance to be covered was ten miles. He had about six months to prepare. His goal was to win the race because the prize money was worth fighting for. He decided to train his body to get accustomed to long-distance running. The first day he set out, he was only able to run about three miles. He continued this every other day for one week with little or no success. But he persevered. By the fifth week, he was running ten miles comfortably. Then by the sixth week, he reasoned with himself that if he must win the race, he must get used to running at least twenty miles at a time. So, he started running twenty miles every other day. At first, it seemed impossible. But as he continued, he was able to comfortably run twenty miles every other day. He continued with this pattern until the day of the race. Of course, he won the race. He'd prepared very well for it, and his efforts paid off.

Now then, imagine if this same young man was not sure of the

33

distance to be covered in the marathon race. And he decided to practice running only three miles, only to find out on the D-day that the distance to be covered is ten miles. Definitely, he will stand no chance. He will be lucky if he finishes the race. Again, imagine if the young man practices running exactly ten miles. He might finish the race, but his winning the first place is not guaranteed. This principle applies to almost every area of life where success is required. I do not think it will be any different when it comes to preparing for the end time. Knowing what you are likely to encounter puts you in a better preparatory position. Being uncertain about the timing of rapture is like the young man who doesn't know the total distance set for the marathon race. There is no way we can adequately prepare for it. If organizers of such events, which have no eternal value, can think it right to tell the participant what to expect days before, I think God can do far better than any organizer of any event on earth.

Few reasons why it is extremely important for us to know the exact timing of it:

During one of His last sermons before leaving the earth, the disciples asked Jesus about the timing of the rapture. Jesus didn't tell them they were not supposed to know. Jesus answered the question. This means we are expected to know the timing. Let's take a look at the incidence in Matthew 24:3–4:

3. And as he sat upon the mount of Olives, the disciples

34

came unto him privately, saying, Tell us, when shall
these things be? and what shall be the sign of thy
*coming, and of the end of the world? 4. **And Jesus***
***answered** and said unto them, Take heed that no man*
deceive you.

Did you notice the questions the disciples ask? Let's break the
questions down. The first question they ask is: Tell us, when shall
these things be? Did you notice a question mark at the end of that first
question? It shows that this is a question and it therefore requires
Jesus to answer. Look at the second statement that follows: And what
shall be the sign of Thy coming and of the end of the world? Did you
also notice another question mark at the end of that statement? So,
what do the questions mean? The first question is about the matter of
the destruction of the temple. In Verse 1 of this same chapter, Jesus
has talked about a time in history when the temple will be completely
destroyed. Look at it: Matthew 24:1–2:

1. And Jesus went out, and departed from the temple:
and his disciples came to him for to shew him the
buildings of the temple. 2. And Jesus said unto them,
See ye not all these things? verily I say unto you, There
shall not be left here one stone upon another, that shall
not be thrown down.

Then, when the disciples find a convenient time, they ask the three-in-one question: When shall the temple be destroyed? When is the second coming going to be? When is the day of the Lord going to be? Can you see those three questions in the passage above? Look at it again. The second question asks, What shall be the sign of your coming? What is that? That is the second coming. Look at the third: What shall be the sign of the end of the world? What is that? The day of the Lord. Now then, Jesus was to answer this question. Look at what Verse 4 starts with: Matthew 24:4:

> *4. And Jesus answered and said unto them, Take heed that no man deceive you.*

The verse starts with "And Jesus answered" . . . meaning He decided to answer the question. It also means that whatever Jesus says after that is an attempt to answer the question. You might say, "Oh no, Jesus is so meek, He won't want to say no, he will just try to be diplomatic in order not to offend them." I don't think that is the case here. Jesus, at the start of His ministry, warns that anything beyond yes or no can be from a sinful heart: Matthew 5:37:

> *37. But let your communication be, Yea, yea; Nay, nay: for whatsoever is more than these cometh of evil.*

That will be equating Him to the pharisees who say but don't act. Searching through the New Testament, we have seen at least three situations where Jesus refuses to answer direct questions. Look at one of the scenarios in Act 1:6–7:

> *6. When they therefore were come together, **they asked of him**, saying, Lord, wilt thou at this time restore again the kingdom to Israel? 7. And he said unto them, It **is not for you to know** the times or the seasons, which the Father hath put in his own power.*

Did you notice that Jesus doesn't answer the question? Did you also notice that Jesus tells them straight up that they don't need to know about that? No dribbling. But in the case of Mathew 24, Jesus answers the question directly. Now what does that mean to us? If Jesus goes straight into answering the question, then He expects us to know. Now then, what kind of questions do they ask? The summary of the questions is, what is it that we will see that will make us know for sure that your coming is here or that rapture is at hand? In other words, will the rapture come before or after the great tribulation? Jesus answers the question eagerly. It is therefore wrong and unscriptural for anyone to say we cannot know the signs that will immediately precede rapture. It is also wrong to say that whatever position you take, God will work with you. As we will see in the latter parts of this book, Jesus was clear about when the rapture will occur. Again, if He was not certain on whether it will be before or after the great tribulation, then He stands in danger of being guilty for breaking the above Scripture (Matthew 5:37). But we all can agree that Jesus did not break any Scripture/law. Therefore, we should expect Him to tell exactly when the rapture will be. If in the church today, there is so much ambiguity about the time, it is not because the Bible is not clear on it, it is because we have allowed the devil to confuse us about the matter.

The second reason why we should strive to know the actual sequence of events with respect to rapture is the first statement Jesus made when answering the questions the disciples asked Him. Look at it in Matthew 24:4:

> *4. And Jesus answered and said unto them, Take heed that no man deceive you.*

The first statement Jesus makes with respect to the timing of the second coming and the day of the Lord is: Take heed that no man deceives you. Why would Jesus start with that out of all there is to say about the issue? This is to tell us that that period will be marked by deception to the extent that if we are to give a title or theme to the events of the end time, we can simply say: deception at its peak. Did you notice the phrase "no man" in that statement? Why does He use that phrase? Why not say, do not let the devil deceive you? It means that the deception about the matter can come from any quarter. It can come from the church and from the world. No man includes male or female, learned or unlearned, Pastors or archbishop, General overseer or superintendent, Professor of theology or professor of eschatology—no man means no man. Even though the root of all

38

deception is the devil, man will be used to deceive many concerning the matters of rapture. Also, for Jesus to warn us about deception means that the consequences of deception can be very dangerous. This is not one of the disciples warning us. This is Christ Himself warning us. The warning is so important that it forms the first statement in His answer to the questions about the second coming and the day of the Lord. If you read down the remaining part of the response (we shall look at it later on in this book), you will also notice that Jesus sounded the warning of not being deceived at least three more times. Can you see how important it is not to be deceived in this matter? The deception that Jesus warned against actually started with the early church. Remember the passage we considered earlier about the church in Thessalonica? That is a clear indication that the devil is going to throw all the weight of his deception trick behind this matter. Therefore, any time spent researching what the Bible says (not any man) about the matter is worthwhile

Another reason why we should bother about the timing is that God has not left us in darkness regarding the timing of the second coming and the day of the Lord. Every prophet in the Old Testament talks directly or indirectly about it. Every book in the New Testament talks about it. It seems as if two-third of the entire prophecies in the Bible are related to this matter. There are overwhelming details concerning the matter of the end in the Bible. A closer look will give you amazing details without a shadow of doubt about what God expects us to know about the matter. If God took great effort to tell several prophets over thousands of years, details about a matter and asked that such details be recorded in a book that we call the Bible, don't you think there will be some form of reprimanding for those who did not take time out to search it out? I believe God is not verbose. If such effort and space is put into a particular topic, I believe heaven wants us to know as many details as possible because knowledge of such details will give us certain advantages over the enemy.

Thirdly, the Bible doesn't tell us the format the mark of the beast will take. It only says it requires wisdom to be able to decode what the mark is. If the actual timing of rapture is post-tribulation and we believe in pre-tribulation, we will continually dismiss any and everything that will take the format of the mark, saying we will be raptured before the mark comes. That is a dangerous position to take. Now, let us imagine that the mark is a kind of computerized chip that can be embedded under the skin of your right hand or your forehead. Let us also imagine that every personal electronic we use today can be packaged into this chip that is underneath your skin. That means there will be no need for credit cards, phone, keys to unlock your cars, your home, your office, etc. Can you imagine how difficult it will be to live in that kind of world without access to such a chip? Little wonder the Bible says that without the chip, you can't buy or sell: Revelation 13:17:

17. And that no man might buy or sell, save he that had

40

the mark, or the name of the beast, or the number of his name.

Can you imagine what that means in our world? You can't work, you can't buy or sell anything. For those that live in countries where mortgage is used to purchase homes, you can't pay your home loan. That means you can be pushed out of your homes. Now where do you go? How do you feed? What if you have infants on formula (milk)? Will you take the mark because of the baby? Now then, imagine that suddenly we are faced with the choice of receiving or rejecting such chips in our body. It will be difficult to make the right choice if you don't know the position of God concerning the timing of rapture. I can imagine that the mark will be well publicized worldwide as a means of saving our world. I can imagine that those who refuse the mark will be seen as enemies of progress of our world. I can imagine that those who refuse the mark will be ostracized from the society, both in physical and virtual world. They will be given a lifetime bind from Facebook, Twitter, YouTube, and Instagram. This is really not hard to imagine. We all have witnessed a precedence just recently. Given this kind of situation, you can make a grave and irrecoverable mistake if in fact such a chip is the mark, and the church is still here while the mark is being enforced. Someone might say, "No one can force me to take anything I don't want to take." I guess it's not too difficult to imagine that that can easily happen given what the world has seen in the last two years. Again, someone might say if he/she takes the mark, God will understand. Her baby is dying, her grandma needs medical attention, his car loan needs to be paid, whatever the reason is. I am sorry to inform you that God will not understand. He already stated clearly in the Scripture that whoever takes the mark is doomed forever: Revelation 14:9–10:

> *9. And the third angel followed them, saying with a loud voice,* ***If any man*** *worship the beast and his image,* ***and receive his mark in his forehead****, or in his hand, 10. The same shall drink of the wine of the wrath of God, which is poured out without mixture into the cup of his indignation; and he shall be tormented with fire and brimstone in the presence of the holy angels, and in the presence of the Lamb.*

Can you see that? If any man means whoever. Regardless of the legitimacy of the reason for taking the mark, once anyone takes the mark, that person is doomed forever. This is a serious issue. This is a good reason for the church to be definite about the timing in order to save many people. If the rapture will not take the church before the mark is introduced into our world, then the majority in the church is going to be in great danger of eternal damnation. Can you imagine that?

Fourthly, there are some matters that are considered weightier matters and others not as weighty. That is not to say that everything mentioned in the Bible is not important. For example, in Matthew

23:23, Jesus says this concerning the Pharisees:

> *23. Woe unto you, scribes and Pharisees, hypocrites! for ye pay tithe of mint and anise and cummin, and have omitted the weightier matters of the law, judgment, mercy, and faith: these ought ye to have done, and not to leave the other undone.*

Looking at that passage, one can see that there are some matters of the law/our walk with God, that has more weight than others. One can also note that in this passage, Jesus is not dismissing the payment of tithe. He is saying it is better to pay your tithe and live a life pleasing to God than to pay your tithe and assume that your payment will help you make heaven without paying attention to a lifestyle that is pleasing to God. I believe rapture is one of those weightier matters. Consider 1 John 3:2–3:

> *2. Beloved, now are we the sons of God, and it doth not yet appear what we shall be: but we know that, when he shall appear, we shall be like him; for we shall see him as he is. 3. And every man that hath this hope in him purifieth himself, even as he is pure.*

The first thing to note in this passage is that it is talking about rapture. We can safely make a point, using this passage, that rapture is a weightier matter of our walk with God. Did you notice that it says

43

every Christian that has the hope of the rapture in him/her purifies himself/herself? If there is anything Christ expects from us, it is to be in a constant state of purification. If the hope of rapture can be part of the things to help you achieve purification, then I think it is a weightier matter of our walk with God. If it is a weightier matter of our walk with God, then not knowing the timing as stated in the Bible is like gambling with one of the most important parts of our walk with God.

Another reason why we must know for sure the position of God concerning rapture is that the Bible tells us that the antichrist will be very charismatic and easily likeable. He will deceive the whole world with his speech. People will actually think he is God. If the church is still here at the time of his showing, many believers will follow him, saying this is definitely not the antichrist since rapture has not taken place. Can you again see why Jesus's opening statement about the matter is "do not be deceived"?

Another reason why we should and must know the timing is because of what happened in His first coming. All the Jewish people were expecting the Messiah to come at His first coming. They expected Him to come in a certain way. They expected Him to deliver them from the oppression of the Roman empire. But they completely missed it. These were men that were supposedly professors of the Scriptures, but they gave their own interpretation to it expecting the Bible to dance to their tune. The Bible should never be read like that.

The Bible is God's word to correct us, and it is not for us to tell the Bible what it should say. Because of their prejudice about the Messiah, they completely missed the day of their visitation. Look at what Jesus says concerning that in Luke 19:41–44:

> *41. And when he was come near, he beheld the city, and wept over it, Saying, 42. If thou hadst known, even thou, at least in this thy day, the things which belong unto thy peace! but now they are hid from thine eyes. 43. For the days shall come upon thee, that thine enemies shall cast a trench about thee, and compass thee round, and keep thee in on every side, 44. And shall lay thee even with the ground, and thy children within thee; and they shall not leave in thee one stone upon another; because thou knewest not the time of thy visitation.*

About forty years after Jesus left, the Jewish people severely suffered for misinterpreting the Scriptures about the Messiah. The temple was completely destroyed. People were killed and crucified to the extent that there was no more wood to crucify any more. In the same way, missing the timing of the second coming can be with grave consequences.

Chapter 4

So far, we have let the Bible speak for itself. There is no ambiguity in any of our explanations. Every one of our conclusions drawn has clearly been derived from every passage we have examined. We haven't drawn out any deeper revelation from any of the passages that will take only the eye of an eagle to see. We have just simply magnified what each of the passages say without adding our own ideas. No additional personal revelation. No deeper revelation from any of the passages that only one person can see, with no allegory. All Scriptures used so far can easily be seen by any Christian at any level of faith.

With that in mind, we are going to take a look at all the passages we can lay our hands on that the pre-, mid-, and post-tribulation rapture doctrines stand on and determine whether they truly reflect the mind of God (what the Bible say) or are human fabrication. We shall start our dealings with the pre- and mid-tribulation doctrine. The reason for dealing with the two doctrines together is that they more or less stand on the same doctrine—rapture takes place before the great tribulation. The only difference between them is that the pre-tribulation doctrine believes that Christians will not see the antichrist, while the mid-tribulation doctrine believes that Christians will see the antichrist for only three and a half years, and just before the great tribulation, which is the second three and a half years in the seven-year reign of the antichrist, rapture will take place. The post-tribulation doctrine stands alone when it comes to the issue of the great tribulation. It is the only doctrine (that I know of) that says that the believers will face the great tribulation. We shall do a study of that later in this book, but for now let's together look at the first two doctrines.

Based on the pre- and mid-tribulation rapture doctrines, the following is a summarized version of the timeline of the matters of rapture:

Rapture of the church will be the first event, after which the antichrist will be revealed. (In the case of the mid-tribulation, the antichrist would have been around for three and a half years before rapture takes place). The antichrist will reign for seven years. In those seven years, Christians that are raptured will be in heaven with Christ for the Lord's supper, which will also last for seven years. The Christians that are left behind will have to suffer punishment from the antichrist. They will have to pay for their own salvation with their blood without the help of the Holy Spirit, as the Holy Spirit would have been taken away from the earth with the church. During those seven years, God will be pouring out His wrath on earth. After the seven-year reign of the antichrist is over, Christ will now come back to the earth, and that is known as the day of the Lord.

Now, let us take a look at some of the passages that these doctrines are hanging on to see if this is the mind of God or some fallacy propagated by humans:

Revelation 3:10 Doctrine

10. Because thou hast kept the word of my patience, I also will keep thee from the hour of temptation, which shall come upon all the world, to try them that dwell upon the earth.

The teaching from this passage is that any Christian who keeps God's word now shall be kept at the time of tribulation by being raptured from the earth just before the great tribulation starts. Now let's take a deeper look at this passage and see if that is what Jesus is trying to communicate to John. First, let's give a background story here. All the disciples of Jesus were considered the enemy of the state initially by the Jewish rulers and then later by the Roman empire. Hence, they suffered persecution. Martyrdom was a common occurrence among Christians in those days because of their faith in Christ. John the apostle was martyred, but he didn't die. So, they sent him on exile to the island of Patmos (Rev 1:9), which was more like a prison island with hard labor. It was at this island that Jesus visited him with the Revelation. Now then, let's consider the context in which Jesus says those words (Rev 3:10). First it must be noted that at the beginning of the conversation between John and Jesus, Jesus clearly states the purpose of the conversation. Look at Revelation 1:1:

1. The Revelation of Jesus Christ, which God gave unto him, to shew unto his servants things which must shortly come to pass; and he sent and signified it by his angel unto his servant John.

Notice how John puts it in that introductory note. It is the Revelation of Jesus that God gave to Him. Second, it is of things that must happen shortly. What shortly means, we don't know. Now notice the instruction given in Revelation 1:19:

19. Write the things which thou hast seen, and the things which are, and the things which shall be hereafter.

The instruction given is to write. Write what? Write the things he has seen in the vision. "The things which are"'; what does that mean? It means the things happening in the days of John. Hence, the revelation that he (John) is to write down from what Jesus will be dictating and showing, is about things happening in his days and things happening in the days to come. Now then, if you look at Revelation 2 from Verse 1, Jesus starts talking to him about the seven churches in his days. They are not imaginary churches or parabolic churches. They are actual churches that existed in the days of John. And the messages Jesus is given are messages that Jesus commanded John to give directly to the leaders of these actual churches. Although we can learn from these instructions, they are meant specifically for those pastors and those churches. Jesus is dishing out the instructions to these churches based on their successes and failures in the ministry at that time (in the days of John). Now if you look at Revelation 3:7–10

> *7. And to the angel of the church in Philadelphia write; These things saith he that is holy, he that is true, he that hath the key of David, he that openeth, and no man shutteth; and shutteth, and no man openeth. 8. I know thy works: behold, I have set before thee an open door, and no man can shut it: for thou hast a little strength, and hast kept my word, and hast not denied my name. 9. Behold, I will make them of the synagogue of Satan, which say they are Jews, and are not, but do lie; behold, I will make them to come and worship before thy feet, and to know that I have loved thee. 10. Because thou hast kept the word of my patience, I also will keep thee from the hour of temptation, which shall come upon all the world, to try them that dwell upon the earth.*

He starts telling John to write down instructions for the pastor in the church of Philadelphia ("the "angel" in that passage refers to the bishop or general overseer (humans) of the church and not the heavenly beings" – Revelation 1:20). Did you notice He starts with "and to the angel . . ."? What does that mean? It means the next sets of statements I will say, you must write them down and send them to the angel of the church in Philadelphia. Hence, looking at the passage from the context, the message is for a specific church located in Philadelphia at the time of John. If you take a trip to Turkey today, the ruins of the city where this church existed, are still standing. And in fact, the ruin of the church itself is now a tourist attraction. Therefore, the message in Revelation 3:10 was originally meant for the church of Philadelphia in the days of John. Yes, we can learn from it, but there is a problem if we base a doctrine of a matter as weighty as rapture on it.

The second problem with this passage (Revelation 3:10) in relation to rapture is that a few years after this prophecy, the time of tribulation that Jesus speaks about in that passage befell that area. It affected the other six churches adversely, but the Philadelphia church survived. Therefore, we cannot equate the hour of tribulation Jesus speaks about concerning the church of Philadelphia to the great tribulation. (It is good to note that all the seven churches mentioned in the book of Revelation are in Turkey and located not very far from each other.)

From what we have seen so far, it means that it was inferred from that passage that God will keep the Christians of this generation from the great tribulation if they keep His word in the same way as He kept the Christians who kept His word in the days of John from the tribulation that befell them. And according to the doctrine, the way God will do that is by taking the church out through rapture. This is another risky thing to do—hanging the weight of a topic as important as rapture on inference. But then, another question will be: is it wrong

to infer from the Scriptures? The answer is NO. Inference from the Scriptures is okay as long as the inference is a true correlation. What does true correlation mean? I will give you an example. In order to get water, you need to combine two molecules of hydrogen gas and one molecule of oxygen gas under certain atmospheric pressure and temperature conditions. If you do that experiment anywhere on earth, as long as the four conditions are met, you will get water. What are these four conditions? You must have two molecules of hydrogen gas, one molecule of oxygen gas, and certain temperature and pressure. Now then, one can safely infer that if you break water down, you will get two molecules of hydrogen gas and one molecule of oxygen gas. That is true inference. But it is not right to say that when you break water down, you get one molecule of hydrogen gas and two molecules of oxygen gas. Someone might say what is the big deal? What matters is that hydrogen and oxygen gases are present, it doesn't matter in what quantity. The problem with that is that, yes, oxygen and hydrogen gases may be present, but the moment the right quantity changes, it is no longer water. It might look like water, but it is not water. So, with this at the back of our minds, let's look at Revelation 3:10 again through the lens of inference:
Revelation 3:10:

10. Because thou hast kept the word of my patience, I also will keep thee from the hour of temptation, which shall come upon all the world, to try them that dwell upon the earth.

Now, looking at the passage, we can safely say that even though this passage was originally meant for the Philadelphian Church in the days of John, if we do what its members did, we can get the result they got. They kept the word of Jesus, and Jesus kept them from the hour of temptation or tribulation. Now let's put a little microscope on the passage and see what Jesus really meant when He said He will keep them from the hour of tribulation. The New Testament was written mostly in Greek. The words "Keep" and "Kept" in the above passage originate from the same Greek word: Tereo (pronounced "tay-reh-o"), which means to guard from loss or injury or prevent from escaping, which implies a fortress or full military lines. It also means to preserve or to keep one in the state in which he is or to take care of. Nothing in the definition of the word implies that to keep means we have to be taken out of the earth by rapture. On the other hand, it actually implies that we should be here during the tribulation but be kept from harm. The Philadelphian Church was not taken out of the world during its hour of tribulation. It was protected by the power of God while in the midst of the tribulation. We therefore cannot apply that passage to us being raptured before the great tribulation. It is not right to base this assumption on just this one passage. Let us look at another passage that used the same word—keep—from the same root word and see what it means. John 17:15:

15. I pray not that thou shouldest take them out of the world, but that thou shouldest keep them from the evil.

53

These words are said by Jesus to His disciples, which also includes us. He uses the same Greek word in this verse. Did you notice what He says? He says to God not to take them out of the world but to *keep* them from the evil. Why does He use the word "the" in front of evil? Because He is probably referring to a person. The evil one. If you check some translations, they put "the evil one" in place of "the evil." In essence, Christ Himself prayed that we be not taken from the earth by rapture but be kept by the power of God throughout the period of trouble. Therefore, the inference of basing Revelation 3:10 on rapture is not right. If we must infer, then we have to infer rightly and safely. If we want to infer rightly and safely, then Revelation 3:10 actually means God should keep us through the period of tribulation and not take us out. It should also be of note that the Christians whom this word was specifically meant for were not taken out of the world during the time of their tribulation and neither were they taken to another part of the country or the earth. They were only kept from being adversely affected by the tribulation while they remained in the city where the tribulation was being unleashed. Why then should we, who are just trying to hold unto the passage that is not originally meant for us, assume that we shall be taken out of the earth in order to be kept from tribulation?

Now then, let us consider another question. Is this consistent with the nature of God or events throughout the Scriptures? The answer is YES. God didn't keep Shadrach, Meshach, and Abednego from entering the fiery furnace of Nebuchadnezzar; He kept them from being consumed in the fire. And we see this consistently through the Scriptures. We shall talk more on this consistency in later chapters.

Chapter 5

Revelation 4:1–4

> *1. After this I looked, and, behold, a door was opened in heaven: and the first voice which I heard was as it were of a trumpet talking with me; which said, Come up hither, and I will shew thee things which must be hereafter. 2. And immediately I was in the spirit: and, behold, a throne was set in heaven, and one sat on the throne. 3. And he that sat was to look upon like a jasper and a sardine stone: and there was a rainbow round about the throne, in sight like unto an emerald. 4. And round about the throne were four and twenty seats: and upon the seats I saw four and twenty elders sitting, clothed in white raiment; and they had on their heads crowns of gold.*

This is another passage frequently used to prove that the church will be raptured before the great tribulation. The doctrine states that when the trumpet is sounded in Verse 1 of the passage, John is immediately raptured into heaven. The doctrine concludes that John represents the church and John, a representation of the church, is raptured before the great tribulation started in Chapter 5 by the opening of the seals. Let's see whether this is what the Bible is trying to communicate to us in the passage.

In order for us to get the truth about this passage, we need to compare it to other passages that clearly speak about rapture and see if there are any similarities. Again, remember the rule: no doctrine is permitted to stand on one Scripture. It must stand on two or three Scriptures in order for it to be established as truth. Now then, when we compare this passage to other passages that describe the rapture, we will notice some very interesting things. In this passage, John hears a person's voice that sounds like a trumpet. Look at it: Revelation 4:1:

> *1. After this I looked, and, behold, a door was opened in heaven: and the first voice which I heard was as it were of a trumpet talking with me; which said, Come up hither, and I will shew thee things which must be hereafter.*

Notice how John puts it in the above passage. The first voice, not the first trumpet. Notice also that the voice is talking and not sounding. John is only trying to describe the voice, that is why he says it sounded like a trumpet. In order to be sure whether what John is saying here is rapture or different from rapture, let's look at the passages that speak of the trumpet sounding to usher in rapture and see whether there is a voice to it: 1 Thessalonians 4:16:

> *16. For the Lord himself shall descend from heaven with a shout, with the voice of the archangel, and with the trump of God: and the dead in Christ shall rise first:*

Notice how Paul puts it in the above passage. This passage doesn't say the trumpet will talk to anyone, neither does it say the trumpet is a voice. Rather, it separates the trumpet from the voice of the archangel and the shout. In Thessalonians 4, a shout, a voice, and a trumpet are talked about. But the passage in Revelation 4:1 talks about a voice that sounds like a trumpet. They are two completely different things. For more clarification, let's look at another passage that describes the trumpet sound in rapture. 1 Corinthians 15:51–52:

> *51. Behold, I shew you a mystery; We shall not all sleep, but we shall all be changed, 52. In a moment, in the twinkling of an eye, at the last trump: for the trumpet shall sound, and the dead shall be raised incorruptible, and we shall be changed.*

Again, the Bible talks about the trumpet sound that will usher in the rapture. But it doesn't mention that there will be a voice or that the trumpet will sound like a voice. Okay, let us assume that in the last two passages, the Bible doesn't mention the voice. And let us also assume that the trumpet that will sound at rapture will be a voice telling Christians to come up. Let's further examine Revelation 4:1 to determine whether what is being described is rapture: Revelation 4:1:

> *1. After this I looked, and, behold, a door was opened in heaven: and the first voice which I heard was as it were of a trumpet talking with me; which said, Come*

up hither, and I will shew thee things which must be
hereafter.

In this passage, it says the voice is the first voice. If we are assuming that the voice is the trumpet, then we are saying that the trumpet that sounds here in Revelation 4 is the first trumpet. But that is completely different from the trumpet that will sound at rapture. 1 Corinthians 15 says it is the last trumpet. They both can't be talking about the same thing. One says the first trumpet and the other says the last trumpet. That's misleading, and I don't believe God would want to mislead us.

Now then, let us again assume that there is no discrepancy between Verse 1 of Revelation 4 and the other passages that talk about rapture that we looked at. Let us see if at least Verse 2 of Revelation 4 will give a better clue to the doctrine: Revelation 4:2:

2. And immediately I was in the spirit: and, behold, a
throne was set in heaven, and one sat on the throned.

Notice the first part of that passage: And immediately I was in the spirit. The passages that talk about rapture don't say we will be in the spirit when rapture takes place. They don't say it will be a spiritual event. Look at it in 1 Corinthians 15:52–53:

52. In a moment, in the twinkling of an eye, at the last

59

trump: for the trumpet shall sound, and the dead shall be raised incorruptible, and we shall be changed. 53. For this corruptible must put on incorruption, and this mortal must put on immortality.

It says here that we shall be changed. We shall have a new body, and with that new body, we shall be with Christ. No part of us will be left. This is completely different from what John describes in Revelation 4. In Revelation 4, John says he was in the spirit. What does that mean? It means his spirit was lifted to heaven while his body was here. This phenomenon is not unique to John. Many other prophets in the Bible have had similar experiences, where they were taken to heaven in the spirit. An example is Isaiah. He appears in heaven in Chapter 6 of the book of Isaiah, and he sees almost the same thing that John does. Look at it in Isaiah 6:1:

1. In the year that king Uzziah died I saw also the Lord sitting upon a throne, high and lifted up, and his train filled the temple.

How does he see the Lord and the throne of God in heaven? We sure know he didn't die. We also know that he didn't see the Lord and the throne with his physical eyes. The only way he could have seen the Lord and the throne of God in heaven is if he was taken in the spirit to heaven. This is the exact same experience John has had. Many other prophets in the Bible have had this same experience.

Therefore, we cannot single the experience of John out because we are trying to create a narrative that the Bible didn't say.

Again, according to 1 Corinthians 15, no part of us will be left. A good reason why we have a new body is so that we can have access to the terrestrial realm because our current body is bound to the earth. The new body will be immortal and incorruptible.

Now then, if we look further into Verse 2 of Revelation 4, we shall discover other discrepancies with other passages that speak about rapture: Revelation 4:2:

> *2. And immediately I was in the spirit: and, behold, a throne was set in heaven, and one sat on the throne.*

In the above passage, the Bible says, immediately John was in the spirit, he found himself in heaven before the throne of God. But that is completely different from what is described about rapture. Look at it here:

> *16. For the Lord himself shall descend from heaven with a shout, with the voice of the archangel, and with the trump of God: and the dead in Christ shall rise first: 17. Then we which are alive and remain shall be caught up together with them in the clouds, to meet the Lord in the air: and so shall we ever be with the Lord.*

This passage doesn't say we shall immediately find ourselves before the throne in heaven. It says we shall be caught up in the clouds to meet the Lord in the air. Someone might say oh Revelation 4 actually skipped that part where we meet the Lord in the air. Then I will say to you that if that is the case, then the Bible lies when it says immediately John found himself in heaven. You and I know that the Bible cannot lie. Revelation 4 would have said after the trumpet sounded, John was in the spirit, and behold, a throne was set in heaven. That would have given us an idea that the Bible deliberately skipped the part where we were in the air with the Lord. But Revelation 4 says immediately . . . which means there was no time John found himself in the cloud or in the air. Look at it again; Revelation 4:1–2:

> *1. After this I looked, and, behold, a door was opened in heaven: and the first voice which I heard was as it were of a trumpet talking with me; which said, Come up hither, and I will shew thee things which must be hereafter. 2.* **And immediately I** *was in the spirit: and, behold, a throne was set in heaven, and one sat on the throne.*

Can you see that? Again, you will notice that the same event happens to John earlier in Chapter 1 of the book of Revelation. Look at it; Revelation 1:10:

> *10. I was in the Spirit on the Lord's day, and heard behind me a great voice, as of a trumpet,*

Can you see that exactly the same thing happens in Chapter four that has also happened in Chapter one? Now then, why should we call what happens in Chapter 4 rapture and ignore what happens in Chapter 1? The two either have to be rapture or the two cannot be rapture. If the two are rapture, then are we saying that rapture occurs twice? The first team went with the rapture in Chapter 1 while the second team went with the rapture in Chapter 4. Which part of the church is the first team and which part is the second? We cannot say that because there is none of the rapture Scriptures that talked about two batches of rapture.

In summary, Revelation 4 cannot be taken to be the rapture of the church because it is completely different from what other passages say about rapture. We cannot infer that John represents the church when there are countless passages that talk directly about the church being raptured. Also, Revelation 4 talks about the first trumpet that ushered John into heaven, but the passages on rapture put it at the last trumpet. Revelation 4 skips the part where the church will be caught up in the air first and says immediately John found himself in heaven, which is contrary to what other passages say about rapture. Revelation 4 says John was in the spirit after the trumpet sounded, which is again contrary to what other passages say about rapture. Then, if you want to take into account that the same experience occurs in Verse 1 of the book of Revelation, then you are saying that rapture occurs twice according to the book of Revelation. We all know that that cannot be true.

Chapter 6

2 Thessalonians 2:7

> *7. For the mystery of iniquity doth already work: only
> he who now letteth will let, until he be taken out of the
> way*

The doctrine around this passage is that the "he" who now letteth is the Holy Ghost. According to the doctrine, the Holy Ghost is the one preventing the antichrist from coming. As long as the Holy Ghost is here, the church will be here, and the antichrist won't be able to come because the Holy Ghost is standing in the way of the antichrist. But at rapture, the Holy Ghost will go with the church, and afterwards, the antichrist will be revealed because He (the Holy Ghost) is now taken out of the way. The doctrine goes on to further say that the Christians that will be left behind will have to get their own salvation using their own blood, as the blood of Jesus will no longer be available for them, and the Holy Ghost will no longer be on earth to help them.

This is the most fascinating of all the doctrines. Let us take a deeper look at the passage to see if this is what the Bible is saying. The base on which this doctrine is hinged is that the "he" that letteth is the Holy Ghost. There is no proof that that "he" is the Holy Ghost. There is no other passage anywhere in the Old or New testaments that says the Holy Ghost is the one holding back the antichrist. Neither is there any passage in the whole of the Bible that says the Holy Ghost will be taken out of the world with the church before the antichrist shows up. A matter of such importance should not stand solely on one Scripture. Let's take a look at 1 John 4:3:

3. And every spirit that confesseth not that Jesus Christ is come in the flesh is not of God: and this is that spirit of antichrist, whereof ye have heard that it should come; and even now already is it in the world.

Notice what John says in this passage. The passage clearly tells us that the spirit of the antichrist has already come into the world. If the doctrine of 1 Thessalonian 1:7 is true, the Holy Ghost, who is also a spirit, should have prevented the spirit of the antichrist from coming into the world until the church was taken away. Even now, the level of decadence we are seeing in our society is what we could never have been able to imagine just ten or fifteen years ago. If someone who is not a believer and had nothing to do with God and who died twenty years ago is miraculously brought back to life to see what our current world has become, he/she will immediately be thrown into convulsion at how appalling our world has become. Why is this so? In the full presence of the church, the spirit of the antichrist has overtaken our society and even crept into our churches. If the doctrine is true, the Holy Ghost will not only stop the antichrist, he will also stop the spirit of the antichrist.

Now then, let us assume that the "he" that is holding back the antichrist from manifesting is the Holy Ghost. In order not to take that passage out of context, let us look at the matter from the beginning of that chapter and see whether Verse 7 fits in the entire chapter or it's a standalone verse. Let us look at what Paul is saying in Verse 1: 2 Thessalonians 1:1–3:

> 1. *Now we beseech you, brethren, by the coming of our Lord Jesus Christ, and by our gathering together unto him, 2. That ye be not soon shaken in mind, or be troubled, neither by spirit, nor by word, nor by letter as from us, as that the day of Christ is at hand. 3. Let no man deceive you by any means: for that day shall not come, except there come a falling away first, and that man of sin be revealed, the son of perdition;*

Did you notice that the first verse mentions the issue Paul was discussing with the Thessalonian Christians? The passage starts with: "Now we beseech you, by the coming of our Lord Jesus Christ" . . . Did you see that in the opening statement of Verse 1? That means that what he is talking about at this point of the letter is related to the second coming of our Lord. Notice also the next phrase that is joined with the first with the word "and." That phrase is referring to the rapture of the church—"and by our gathering together unto Him." Therefore, we can clearly see from the introductory statement of Verse 1 that Paul is about to talk about the second coming of Jesus and Rapture (refer to the section on definition of terms in this book for further clarity). Now then, in the second verse, we can see Paul telling them not to be confused or disturbed by what anyone says, whether it be through a spirit or rumor or even a letter allegedly from himself,

Paul, claiming that the day (rapture) has already come. Now take a closer look at Verse 3. He goes on further to say they should not let anyone deceive them for that day will NOT come until two things happen: the falling away and the revealing of the antichrist. So, here, Paul is telling the church in Thessalonica and us (in extension), that the rapture will not come until the antichrist is revealed. This automatically nullifies the standalone Verse 7 from which the doctrine of rapture was created (the doctrine says the church and the Holy Ghost will be taken away before the antichrist comes). Then it means the "he" spoken about in Verse 7 is not the Holy Ghost. Or else Paul is lying in Verses 1 to 3. Someone might say, "Oh no, you got it mixed up. The day Paul was speaking about in Verses 1 to 3 is the day of the Lord, which is the day that ushers in the wrath of the Lord. It agrees with Verse 7, which says the church has to be taken out of here before the antichrist is revealed and then the wrath is poured out." To this, I will say, "Let us look more closely to the day Paul was referring to again in Verses 1 to 3. I will bring out the words used to describe the day Paul was talking about so you can see for yourself": 2 Thessalonians 2:1–3:

> *1. Now we beseech you, brethren*, **by the coming of our Lord Jesus Christ, and by our gathering together unto him,** *2. That ye be not soon shaken in mind, or be troubled, neither by spirit, nor by word, nor by letter as from us,* **as that the day of Christ** *is at hand. 3. Let no man deceive you by any means*: **for**

that day shall not come, except there come a falling away first, and that man of sin be revealed, the son of perdition;

Can you see the words in bold? The first line says "by the coming of our Lord Jesus Christ." We can easily confuse that to be the day of the Lord. In order for us not to be confused, Paul quickly chips in the second phrase—and by our gathering together unto Him. Can you see that? No one can argue that that second phrase is not rapture. The only event recorded in the Bible where Christians will be caught up or gathered together unto the Lord is rapture. Again, notice how Paul puts it. First, he says "by the coming of our Lord AND our gathering together unto Him." It means that he is referring to one day, not two days. He is referring to two events happening on the same day. The coming of the Lord is the first event, and our gathering together unto Him is the second event. Both events happen on the same day. Can you see that in the above passage? And of course, if you look at some of the passages about rapture we have considered so far, you will see these two events (the coming of the Lord AND our gathering together unto HIM) in them. Let us look at one of them: 1 Thessalonians 4:16–17

*16. For the **Lord himself shall descend** from heaven with a shout, with the voice of the archangel, and with the trump of God: and the dead in Christ shall rise first: 17. **Then we which are alive and remain shall***

> *be caught up together with them in the clouds, to meet the Lord in the air: and so shall we ever be with the Lord.*

No one can argue that the above passage is not speaking about rapture. We are all definitely on the same page with this passage (1 Thessalonian 4:16,17). Now then, look at the highlighted words. Can you see that it is exactly the same picture Paul is trying to paint in 2 Thessalonians 2:1? In 1 Thessalonians 4, Paul is talking about the events that will play out at rapture. Can you see the two events mentioned in 2 Thessalonians 2:1 right in Verses 16 and 17 of 1 Thessalonians 4? The first event is: the Lord Himself will descend. This is exactly what Paul says in 2 Thessalonians but in different words—by the coming of our Lord. Now consider the second statement in both cases. 1 Thessalonians 4 says: we which are alive and remain shall be caught up together, while 2 Thessalonians 2 says: by our gathering together unto him. Can you see that they are both exactly the same thing? Without a shadow of doubt, we can see that what Paul is describing in 2 Thessalonians 2:1 is rapture. Therefore, we shall be wrong if we say the "he" in Verse 7 is the Holy Ghost when Verses 1 to 3 tell us that unless the antichrist is revealed, rapture will not occur.

Another issue with the doctrine of 2 Thessalonian 2:7 is that it affirms that those that will be left behind will be without the Holy Ghost and will pay for their own salvation with their own blood—something along these lines. That, to me is a very major doctrine. This should be mentioned clearly in at least two passages of the Bible. I don't know of any passage in the Bible that affirms that statement or even says something close. On the other hand, there are many passages in the Bible that say the contrary. Let's consider some of them: John 16:13:

> *13. Howbeit when he, the Spirit of truth, is come, he will guide you into all truth: for he shall not speak of himself; but whatsoever he shall hear, that shall he speak: and he will shew you things to come.*

One of the functions of the Holy Ghost in the life of a believer is to guide us into all truth. From what the Bible says about the time of the reign of the antichrist, it will be filled with deception. John gives us a glimpse of what it will be like in those days: Revelation 13:13–14

> *13. And he doeth great wonders, so that he maketh fire come down from heaven on the earth in the sight of men, 14. And deceiveth them that dwell on the earth by the means of those miracles which he had power to do in the sight of the beast; saying to them that dwell on the earth, that they should make an image to the beast, which had the wound by a sword, and did live.*

The deception at that time will be unprecedented. It will be difficult, if not impossible, to discern what is true or untrue. The reason why people will be deceived is because they don't know of any reason why it shouldn't be true. And remember, in the opening statement of Christ when He is answering the question about the signs of the end time, He starts by saying "do not be deceived.": Mathew 24:4:

> *4. And Jesus answered and said unto them, Take heed that no man deceive you.*

Hence, if we were to give a title to the events of the end time or the period of reign of the antichrist, it will be: DECEPTION. Deception is basically defined as making a false narrative to be accepted as true. We can already see that in our world. Even now when the Holy Ghost, the Spirit of truth, is still with us, many Christians are still being deceived into accepting false narratives as true. Now how do you think the believer can discern between true or false at a time when deception is at its peak in human history, without the presence of the Holy Ghost who alone guides us into all truth? It doesn't add up. And according to the doctrine, these are supposed believers who did not take their walk with God seriously when the devil was not at "his best" and when they had the help of the Holy Ghost at their disposal. Now, at the peak of deception, when the devil is given a completely free hand to operate, without the presence of the Holy Ghost, these unserious Christians will suddenly become serious and be able to decipher what is true or false and be able to decode all the tricks of the devil and overcome all tribulation to stand for Christ. I find that hard to believe. Take note that according to the doctrine, they missed the rapture because they gave in to the lies of the devil and considered other things more important than their walk with God. And this was done when the Spirit of truth was at their disposal. Now that the Spirit of truth is gone, they will suddenly realize their mistakes and easily overcome the lies of the devil. Let's look at a biblical example to see whether this theorem will hold: Matthew 26:69–70:

> *69. Now Peter sat without in the palace: and a damsel came unto him, saying, Thou also wast with Jesus of Galilee. 70. But he denied before them all, saying, I know not what thou sayest.*

This is the story of a man who was very passionate about Jesus. He lived with Jesus for three and a half years. He saw miracles and actually performed some himself. He was ready to defend Christ with his very life. But he could not help but deny Jesus before a maid. Was it because he wanted to deny Jesus? The answer is NO. It was because he had no strength to stand. Now let's look at the same Peter after he received strength from the Holy Ghost: Act 2:14:

> *14. But Peter, standing up with the eleven, lifted up his voice, and said unto them, Ye men of Judaea, and all ye that dwell at Jerusalem, be this known unto you, and hearken to my words:*

He stood before thousands of people and boldly declared the very man—Jesus, whom he had denied before one maid because the Holy Ghost strengthened him. Can you see that this is the direct opposite of what the doctrine says? I sincerely do not know how men who could not stand at the time of peace, when the Holy Ghost was available, will be able to stand at the time of the greatest trouble humanity will ever know.

Someone might say, "But the Old Testament saints did great wonders for God, and they didn't have the Holy Ghost." To them I will say that although they were not baptized with the Holy Ghost as those of the New Testament, every exploit they did was through the power of the Holy Ghost. This is the difference between Spirit on and Spirit within. The Old Testament saints have the "Spirit on" and the "Spirit with," while the New Testament saints have the "Spirit on," "Spirit with," and "Spirit in." The full explanation of these phenomena is beyond the scope of this book. Hence, we can clearly conclude that even in the Old Testament, none of the deeds were done without the Holy Ghost.

Another issue that is not right about the 2 Thessalonians 1:7 doctrine is the fact that it concludes that there is no more "regular" salvation for the Christians left behind. They will have to buy their own salvation with their own blood by being killed by the antichrist. The problem with this postulation is that no other blood is good enough to save anyone other than the blood of Jesus. If our blood was good enough, Jesus wouldn't have come. Look at how Paul puts it in Hebrews 9:24–26:

> *24. For Christ is not entered into the holy places made with hands, which are the figures of the true; but into heaven itself, now to appear in the presence of God for us: 25. Nor yet that he should offer himself often, as the high priest entereth into the holy place every year with blood of others; 26. For then must he often have suffered since the foundation of the world: but now once in the end of the world hath he appeared to put away sin by the sacrifice of himself.*

The only sacrifice good enough to put away sin once and for all is the sacrifice of Jesus. No other sacrifice will be accepted for the remission of sin. Look at how Peter puts it in Act 4:12:

> *12. Neither is there salvation in any other: for there is none other name under heaven given among men, whereby we must be saved.*

There is no salvation in any other than in Jesus. So, it is completely against the Scripture to say that someone's blood is good enough to buy him salvation. And this same person was familiar with Christianity when the blood of Jesus was available and couldn't take advantage of it.

In conclusion, the doctrine of 2 Thessalonians 1:7 has no proven base in the Scripture either as a standalone verse or in conjunction with other verses. It is therefore dangerous for us to base such a great matter as the rapture of the church on a doctrine that has no scriptural bearing.

Chapter 7

Matthew 24:37

> *37. But as the days of Noe were, so shall also the coming of the Son of man be.*

Luke 17:28

> *28. Likewise also as it was in the days of Lot; they did eat, they drank, they bought, they sold, they planted, they builded;*

The doctrine built on the basis of these two passages is that, like in the days when God destroyed the earth with flood, Noah the righteous and his family were saved from the flood, so also will the church be saved. Noah and his family represent the church. God saved them from the flood, and He will similarly take the church out of the world, through rapture, in order to save it from the great tribulation the antichrist will bring. Also, when Sodom was destroyed with fire and brimstone, Lot the righteous and his two daughters were saved. Similarly, God will save the church via rapture just before the antichrist comes to unleash his terror on the earth. Let's take a closer look at the passages on which this doctrine stands to see whether that is truly what the Bible is saying. Let's start with Matthew 24:37:

> *37. But as the days of Noe were, so shall also the coming of the Son of man be.*

Notice that Jesus is making a comparison here, and the comparison is between two specific events. He is comparing a specific event that took place in the days of Noah and Lot to a specific event that will take place in the end time. In a broader sense, He is trying to explain something by using what we are all familiar with, that happened in the past, to make us aware of how exactly it will happen in the future. History, they say, always repeats itself. I guess this was the principle Christ was trying to use to create an imagination in our mind about how that period will be. Whatever the case is, the bottom-line is that Jesus is trying to compare the old with which we are familiar with to the new, which we have not yet seen, in order to create a picture of what we should expect so as to be able to adequately carry out the instructions that follow. In order to get the full picture of what Jesus is trying to paint in our hearts, we first have to find out what specific event in the past He is trying to compare to an event in the future. Secondly, we also need to know the specific event in the future He is trying to compare to that in the past. That is the only way to get the exact picture Jesus is trying to paint. And unless we get the picture, we cannot take heed of the instructions that follow. To do this, we cannot stick to one verse alone; if we do, we stand in danger of taking the text out of context. We have to look at the verses before and after. Matthew 24:36–39:

> *36. But of that day and hour knoweth no man, no, not the angels of heaven, but my Father only. 37. But as the days of Noe were, so shall also the coming of the Son of man be. 38. For as in the days that were before the flood they were eating and drinking, marrying and*

giving in marriage, until the day that Noe entered into the ark, 39. And knew not until the flood came, and took them all away; so shall also the coming of the Son of man be.

Notice what Verse 36 says: But of that day and hour knows no man . . . What could this be referring to? It is referring to the "when" (day and hour) and not the "what" (the event of that day). These are two completely different things. Notice that the specific thing in the future that Jesus is trying to use as a basis of comparison to that of the past is the time the event will happen. Note that it is not talking about the event itself. It is talking about the suddenness, unexpectedness, and unanticipated nature of the event. Did you notice that in the first statement in the above verses? Now then, look at the next verse, Verse 37. It compares the days of Noah to the coming of the Son of man. Notice that it doesn't compare the days of Noah to the day of the coming of the Lord or the days of the coming of the Lord. He compares the days of Noah to the coming of the Lord. Then He goes specific in Verses 38 and 39. He says, to paraphrase, they went on with their life affairs and were not aware that destruction was coming until it came. Can you see that? Then He compares the unawareness of the unbelievers of the days of Noah to the unawareness of the people (unbelievers) that will be alive at His coming.

In essence, Jesus is trying to communicate to us that just like the people in the days of Noah went about their daily life without care, not knowing what would befall them, then suddenly, unexpectedly, the flood came, so also, unexpectedly, will that day come upon the people in the end time. Also, just like the people in the days of Lot were going about their daily lives without the slightest hint about what was coming, and suddenly destruction hit them, so also will it be in the end. Can you see that clearly in the passage? This is completely different from the doctrine expounded from these two passages, which says: What Jesus is saying in those passages is that just as Noah and Lot were brought out of the environment they were in before God caused rain and fire and brimstone to destroy their then world, so also will God take the church out of the earth through rapture before the great tribulation starts. Can you see clearly that Jesus isn't saying or never said that? Can you now see that what Jesus is saying is completely different from what the doctrine is built on? Let's look at it another way. Consider these two statements: Jesus saying for as in the days of Noah . . . Noah was saved from the destruction brought about by the flood while the unbelievers perished, and He says, for as in the days of Noah, while Noah entered the ark, the unbelievers knew not until the flood came. Can you see that those are two different things? Both statements have different areas of focus. The focus of the first statement is on Noah being saved from the flood by entering into the ark while the focus of the second statement is on the unbelievers being oblivious of what was going on until the flood destroyed them. The area Jesus is trying to focus on by using this analogy is how the day of the event will be like a thief in the night for the unbelievers.

79

Another problem with the doctrine is that, you will notice that the destruction brought upon the people in the days of Noah and in the days of Lot was brought about by God Himself, and it was unleashed on the unbelievers. But the tribulation that the doctrine claims we shall be saved from will be brought upon the believers by the antichrist. The first was as a result of the wrath of God on people who refused to repent of their sin and the second will be brought upon the people who refuse to denounce their faith. There is no correlation between the two. Hence, it is completely off to compare the two (refer to the section on definition of terms for more clarification).

Another question we need to ask ourselves is, is this consistent with the teaching of the Bible—the unbelievers being oblivious to the day? Let's see some Scriptures: 1 Thessalonians 5:2–3:

> *2. For yourselves know perfectly that the day of the Lord so cometh as a thief in the night. 3. For when they shall say, Peace and safety; then sudden destruction cometh upon them, as travail upon a woman with child; and they shall not escape*

Did you notice how Paul puts it here? Can you see that it is not different in meaning from how Jesus puts it in Matthew 24:36–39? Can you see that the bottom-line of both passages (Matthew 24:36–39 and 1 Thessalonians 5:2–3) is that destruction will come upon them when they least expect it? Now let's look at the second passage: Luke 17:28–30:

80

28. Likewise also as it was in the days of Lot; they did eat, they drank, they bought, they sold, they planted, they builded; 29. But the same day that Lot went out of Sodom it rained fire and brimstone from heaven, and destroyed them all. 30. Even thus shall it be in the day when the Son of man is revealed.

If we were to state the main idea of the short write-up above (Luke 17:28–30), it is clear to all that the main idea of the write-up is the second part of Verse 29: it rained fire and brimstone from heaven and destroyed them all. We can see also from these verses that Jesus is trying to compare how the citizens of Sodom were destroyed to how it will be when He returns. Therefore, it is not appropriate to create a picture that Jesus didn't create in using those past events. The doctrine places its emphasis on Lot escaping the fire and brimstone brought upon Sodom and Gomorrah as a picture of the church escaping the great tribulation. In that aspect, the doctrine is unscriptural. In the latter part of this book, we shall expatiate more on why Jesus used the analogy. For now, let us look at other doctrines

Another problem with the doctrine is that it misinterprets wrath for tribulation. What happened to Sodom and Gomorrah and the people in the days of Noah is not tribulation. It is God's wrath. The people in the days of Lot and the days of Noah sinned against heaven, and heaven reacted by destroying them because there were not enough righteous people in the cities to prevent God's wrath from descending upon them. Let's take the cases one by one again and see if it is tribulation or wrath.

Now then, let us start our search with the people in the days of Noah. When the sin of the people reached its crescendo, God's heart was broken. He had a conversation with the only righteous man at that time. Here is part of the conversation: Genesis 6:13:

> *13. And God said unto Noah, The end of all flesh is come before me; for the earth is filled with violence through them; and, behold, I will destroy them with the earth.*

Can you see that? The conclusion of the matter is to destroy all. That is not tribulation. That is birth from God's wrath brought about by unrepentant hearts. The only solution at this time is to pour wrath upon the people. Was there a preacher to warn them about their sin? Why would God pour His wrath without adequate warnings? The answer to those question is our God is a righteous and fair judge. He will not pour His wrath without adequate warnings. Noah, being the only righteous man, warned the people over and over again about their sin and the consequences, but they refused to pay heed. Look at it in 2 Peter 2:5:

> *5. And spared not the old world, but saved Noah the eighth person, a preacher of righteousness, bringing*

in the flood upon the world of the ungodly;

In the above passage, Noah is called a preacher of righteousness. A preacher is not just a believer. A preacher is a believer who makes an attempt to share his faith with others in order to get them to believe.

Now then, with the little study we have done about the event that happened in the days of Noah, we can see clearly that it meets (100 percent) the definition of the wrath of God and does not fit into the description of tribulation for the following reasons:

First, the people continued to sin despite several warnings from God of their unrighteousness. Second, the anger of God was kindled and the judgement was brought upon all sinners. Third is that all of the unrepentant sinners actually died as a result of the judgment brought upon them.

Therefore, we can make two statements based on what we have considered on the issue of the days of Noah. The first is a biblical fundamentally wrong statement—it is not right to say that just as Noah was saved from the **wrath of God** during the days of Noah, so also the Christians will be saved from the **great tribulation** during the reign of the antichrist. Rather, it is right to say that just as Noah was saved from the **wrath of God** during his days, so shall the believers be saved from the coming **wrath of God** at the end time. Hence, we can confidently say that the doctrine of Matthew 24:37 was built on the first statement, which is a fundamentally unbiblical principle. If it is built on the second statement, which is a biblically fundamental principle, then it will automatically go against the pre-tribulation theorem.

Now then, let us also consider whether the case of Lot is fit to be called tribulation or wrath of God. Again, just like in the days of Noah, God had a conversation with one of the righteous men around during the days of Lot to see if the people can be spared. Let us look at some of it: Genesis 18:20–21:

> *20. And the LORD said, Because the cry of Sodom and Gomorrah is great, and because their sin is very grievous; 21. I will go down now, and see whether they have done altogether according to the cry of it, which is come unto me; and if not, I will know.*

Can you see the above conversation between God and Abraham? The sin of the people is so grievous that it has reached heaven. God has to put a stop to it. The final resort by heaven to put a stop to sin is for God to pour out His wrath and not to bring tribulation. After several warnings, the final resort is to pour His judgment (wrath of God) upon the people. It is His principle to spare the righteous when He does that.

In conclusion, if we are to make any comparison, it has to be based on scripturally established principles. God's wrath is not meant for believers, while tribulation is targeted towards believers.

Chapter 8

Deuteronomy 4:30

When thou art in tribulation, and all these things are come upon thee, even in the latter days, if thou turn to the LORD thy God, and shalt be obedient unto his voice;

Jeremiah 30:7

Alas! for that day is great, so that none is like it: it is even the time of Jacob's trouble; but he shall be saved out of it.

The doctrine around these two passages is that, yes, there is going to be a great tribulation unleashed by the antichrist upon God's people, but the God's people being referred to here are the Israelites. The Christians will not be part of the tribulation. Only the Israelites will suffer persecution because they rejected Jesus.

Let's search out some Scriptures to see how true this doctrine is. According to Daniel's end time vision, the entire period encompassing end-time matters will be of seventy weeks. Look at it here: Daniel 9:24:

24. Seventy weeks are determined upon thy people and upon thy holy city, to finish the transgression, and to make an end of sins, and to make reconciliation for iniquity, and to bring in everlasting righteousness, and to seal up the vision and prophecy, and to anoint the most Holy.

Notice what the Angel Gabriel tells Daniel after his three weeks of prayer and fasting for his people, the Israelites (the people of God). Seventy weeks are determined upon your people . . . What are the seventy weeks for? The angel clearly explains to Daniel what the seventy weeks are for. Look at the passage again. The following reasons are the reasons the angel gives for the seventy weeks: (1) to finish the transgression, (2) to make an end of sin, (3) to make reconciliation for iniquity, (4) to bring in everlasting righteousness, (5) to seal up the vision and prophecy, and (6) to anoint the most Holy. Take a good look at these six reasons for the seventy weeks being determined upon Israel. Can you see that they are more or less the mission of Jesus in His first and second coming? Let us try to take few of the above six points and see whether they apply to Israel alone.

To make reconciliation for iniquity

That phrase sounds familiar. What does the phrase mean? It means to cancel sin or to disannul or forgive or cleanse sin. It also means to make atonement for sin, to purge sin. The definition makes it more familiar. Now let's search through the Scriptures to see if the above phrase applies only to the Jews or to the people that are called by His name, whether Jews or gentiles; Romans 5:10:

> *10. For if, when we were enemies, we were reconciled to God by the death of his Son, much more, being*

reconciled, we shall be saved by his life.

Can you see that that was exactly what Jesus came to do the first time He came? He came to make atonement for our sins and reconcile us to God. Does that apply only to the Jews? Someone might say, "Oh no, the book of Romans was written by Paul for the Jews who resided in Rome; hence this passage still refers to the Jews alone." Alright, let's check out another passage. 2 Corinthians 5:18–19:

> *18. And all things are of God, who hath reconciled us to himself by Jesus Christ, and hath given to us the ministry of reconciliation; 19. To wit, that God was in Christ, reconciling the world unto himself, not imputing their trespasses unto them; and hath committed unto us the word of reconciliation.*

Here, we have a book written by the same Paul, but this time, he wrote it for the gentiles. Did you notice that it says God reconciled us to Himself through Jesus Christ? The reconciliation is not limited to the Jews. The invitation is open to every human on earth. Can you see that in the passage? Therefore, even though the passage in Daniel 9:24 says seventy weeks is determined for thy people (Israel), the moment Jesus comes into the picture, we are grafted into the equation, and we become part of the people of God (Israel) as Jesus has opened the citizenship to us too. You see, it is just like countries like America, which have opened their borders to all. Every one of us originally came from a different nationality. But the government of America graciously took us under its wings. The original people born here are not more American than I am, even though I am an immigrant. The same exact benefits they get as citizens of this great country are available to me as an immigrant-turned-citizen. I am not treated as a second-class citizen because I am an immigrant. I have the same rights as the people originally born here. If the governments of this world can be that fair in their dealings with their citizens, do you think the God who is the judge of the whole earth will be any less fair? We have been brought into the family of Israel through our Lord Jesus Christ. Every benefit Israel has is automatically and equally extended to us. Every challenge that will come the way of Israel in these last days will come our way too because we are Israelites. Don't take my word for it. Let us look it out in the Scripture. Ephesians 2: 11–13:

> *11. Wherefore remember, that ye being in time past Gentiles in the flesh, who are called Uncircumcision by that which is called the Circumcision in the flesh made by hands; 12. That at that time ye were without Christ, being aliens from the commonwealth of Israel, and strangers from the covenants of promise, having no hope, and without God in the world: 13. But now in Christ Jesus ye who sometimes were far off are made nigh by the blood of Christ.*

Wow. Just look at that. It says in Christ Jesus, through the blood of Jesus, we have been brought near. What could that mean? It means through the blood of Jesus, we are no longer aliens to the commonwealth of Israel nor strangers from the covenants of promise. That sounds vague. Let me use what we can understand to give an analogy. When immigrants come into America, they file for citizenship depending on their situation. There are some categories called resident aliens. Meaning they have a permanent residence in the country, but they don't have citizenship. They don't have access to certain benefits that citizens have access to. But notice that the passage says we are no longer aliens, meaning we now have our citizenship through the blood of Jesus. Meaning we are also 100 percent God's people and have access to the same exact benefits that the other God's people (Israel) have access to. That automatically makes us part of the seventy weeks of Daniel's vision and part of Jeremiah 30:7 and Deuteronomy 4:30.

Now then, let's look at another phrase from Daniel 9:24:

and to make an end of sins

The first coming of Jesus did not make an end to sin. The second coming will complete that. At the second coming, we shall have the ultimate salvation from sin. We shall take on a new body that will give us complete victory over sin and death. Let's look at some Scriptures to help our understanding. Hebrews 9:28:

28. So, Christ was once offered to bear the sins of many; and unto them that look for him shall he appear the second time without sin unto salvation.

Here, we see that the first appearance of Christ was to bear the sins of many. But His second appearance is not to bear sin but to bring us to His ultimate salvation where we become incorruptible and sinless. Jesus is not coming to put a complete end to the sins of the Jews alone. Did you notice the choice of words used in Part B of the passage above? And unto them that look for Him . . . Not just the Jewish people, but all who are called by His name, whether Jews or Gentiles. While we are here on earth, we are still subject to making mistakes either by omission or by commission. Sometimes, not doing what we know to be good can be accounted as a sin to us. However, while we are on earth, and still waiting for the final salvation, the Lord in His infinite mercy has made provision for such errors. Look at it in 1 John 1:9:

9. If we confess our sins, he is faithful and just to forgive us our sins, and to cleanse us from all unrighteousness.

This is not a license to sin. For we know that he that has the seed of God in Him cannot sin, just as the Bible says. Look at how John puts it in 1 John 3:9:

9. Whosoever is born of God doth not commit sin; for his seed remaineth in him: and he cannot sin, because he is born of God.

Whosoever is born of God cannot sin. The phrase "cannot sin" means that the person cannot make a habit of sin. The person will be so uncomfortable in sin that he/she won't want to remain in it, just like a fish won't want to remain out of water. That's a confirmation that the seed of God is in that individual. The spirit of the man can never know any sin; the problem is with the soul. The individual now needs to get his/her soul to conform to the word of God. This is a process. This is what Christ will ultimately save us from.

Let's take one more phrase from Daniel 9:24 and see who it applies to, for in the mouth of two or three witnesses, every word is established.

to anoint the most holy:

In the first coming, Jesus came as a lamb to die for the remission of our sins. Look at how John puts it; John 1:29:

29. The next day John seeth Jesus coming unto him, and saith, Behold the Lamb of God, which taketh away the sin of the world.

Did you notice what John the Baptist says about the first coming of Jesus? He came to take away the sin of the world, not the sin of the Jews. Therefore, at His first coming, Jesus came to take away the sin of the world—of both Jews and Gentiles. It is a case of whosoever. Now then, at the second coming, He will be coming as the LION. The King. The anointed One, who is the most Holy, will be anointed as King forever. Daniel 7:13–14:

> *13. I saw in the night visions, and, behold, one like the Son of man came with the clouds of heaven, and came to the Ancient of days, and they brought him near before him. 14. And there was given him dominion, and glory, and a kingdom, that all people, nations, and languages, should serve him: his dominion is an everlasting dominion, which shall not pass away, and his kingdom that which shall not be destroyed.*

From the above passage, we can see that Jesus is coming the second time, not as a lamb that takes away the sin of the world but as a Lion to rule all people, nations, and languages. To the expansion of His kingdom, there is no end.

Now then, going back to Daniel 9:24, even though we only discussed three of the six points highlighted for the seventy weeks appointed for Israel, we can see that it doesn't only apply to the Israelites in flesh, it also applies to the new breed of Israeli citizens engrafted into the nation's commonwealth by the blood of Jesus.

93

Now let's go back to the original passage: Deuteronomy 4:30 and Jeremiah 30:7. The entire book of Deuteronomy is more or less the farewell speech of Moses to the children of Israel. Look at the introductory verse of Deuteronomy: Deuteronomy 1:1

> *1. These be the words which Moses spake unto all Israel on this side Jordan in the wilderness, in the plain over against the Red sea, between Paran, and Tophel, and Laban, and Hazeroth, and Dizahab.*

Hence, the most part of the book of Deuteronomy comprises of Moses trying to tell the Israelites what to expect and how to conduct themselves in the new land they are going into. Now, with that at the back of your mind, consider what he says to them in Chapter 4:30:

> *30. When thou art in tribulation, and all these things are come upon thee, even in the latter days, if thou turn to the LORD thy God, and shalt be obedient unto his voice.*

Now then, it is clear that that verse is talking about the great tribulation coming up at the end time. The doctrine says that the great tribulation is only for the Israelites because this speech is specifically meant for the Jewish people. Worse still, the one in Jeremiah 30:7 specifically refers to it as the time of Jacob's trouble:

94

7. Alas! for that day is great, so that none is like it: it is even the time of Jacob's trouble; but he shall be saved out of it.

Hence, according to the doctrine, the great tribulation is specifically meant for the Jewish people. Now then, from the analysis of the seventy weeks of Daniel in Daniel 9:24, we can clearly see that the great tribulation is not only for Israel. The church is also part of Jacob; therefore, the trouble is not just for Jewish people but for all those who have been brought into the commonwealth of Israel (Jacob) through the blood of Jesus. Let's see another reason why this Jacob's trouble is not just for Israelites alone. Galatians 3:14:

14. Christ hath redeemed us from the curse of the law, being made a curse for us: for it is written, Cursed is every one that hangeth on a tree.

That passage says Christ as redeemed us from the curse of the law. I have a few questions to ask here. First, who is us? Us is not just the Jewish people but all who trust in the saving power of God. Now then, the next question is, what is the curse of the law? The curse of the law can be read in Deuteronomy 28:15–68. This is part of the farewell speech Moses gave to the children of Israel. The exact same speech where he talked about the great tribulation coming to Israel in later days. So, can we say we have been redeemed from the curse of the law and will not be partakers of the great tribulation coming to Israel? Are we just redeemed from the curse of the law and set apart from Israel? Someone might say, "Oh no, the tribulation is for Israel because they refused to accept Jesus." I have a few questions along that line too. Do you know Christianity didn't come to us Gentiles until at least ten years after the resurrection of Christ? The three thousand people that were born again at Pentecost; do you think they were Gentiles? No, they were all Jews. The five thousand people added to the church in Act 4:4; do you think there was any Gentile among them? No, they were all Jews. Now do you mean to say that the moment the Gentiles came into the fold, the Jewish people stopped accepting Jesus? No, even more accepted Him. Even today, we have millions of Jews scattered all over the world who believe in Jesus. Does the doctrine hold in this case, or does it need to be reviewed? What will the review be? That all the Jewish people who are born again will go with the church, and the non-born again Jews will remain and suffer the great tribulation? That's more or less saying the great tribulation is for all unbelievers, which automatically nullifies the doctrine.

Chapter 9

Daniel 3:8–29

The doctrine coined out of this passage is as follows: when Nebuchadnezzar set up his image so the then world under his rule must worship it, Daniel was missing the entire time. The Bible doesn't mention Daniel, neither does it tell us his whereabouts. Daniel, according to the doctrine, is said to be a picture of the church, which will not be around when the antichrist will be reigning. Just as Daniel is not mentioned in the entire event that plays out concerning the image Nebuchadnezzar sets up, so the church will be raptured just before the antichrist unleashes his terror on the earth. Daniel's companions, the three Hebrew boys—Shadrach, Meshach and Abednego—are a representation of the part of the church that will be left behind. They will be forced to face the tribulation of the antichrist by being thrown into the fiery furnace.

This is a very interesting doctrine. There are a couple of things that make this doctrine unscriptural. First, why is it that the three companions of Daniel are left behind? Does the Bible say rapture will be selective with those that will be taken? (Some will be taken and some will be left)? Let's look at the passage where Paul describes the event and see how it is framed. 1 Thessalonians 4:16–17:

> *16. For the Lord himself shall descend from heaven with a shout, with the voice of the archangel, and with the trump of God: and the dead in Christ shall rise*

first: 17. Then we which are alive and remain shall be
caught up together with them in the clouds, to meet the
Lord in the air: and so shall we ever be with the Lord.
Wherefore comfort one another with these words.

That passage clearly lays out the sequence of events that will take place at rapture. Let us look at it together. First, the Lord Jesus Christ will descend from heaven with a shout, with a voice of the archangel, and with a trumpet of God. Then those who are dead in Christ will rise first. "We which are alive" will be the next to rise. It doesn't say some of the dead will rise and neither does it say some of us who are alive will meet with Christ in the air. It says "we which are alive and remain." This means all true believers who are alive will go. None will be left behind. But in this case, three righteous men are left behind and only one is taken. That is, only 25 percent of the total body of Christ will be taken at rapture (according to the doctrine). That is what I will call selective rapture. What is the basis of selection? Will the pastors and Bishops and church leaders be the 25 percent that will be taken and the rest of the church be the 75 percent that will be left behind? There is no passage in the Bible wherein rapture is described as being a selective event. And even if there was such a passage, the Bible would have at least given us the criteria for the selection. On that basis, we can declare this inference unscriptural.

Now then, maybe we should look at the doctrine from another angle. What if the doctrine assumes that the three companions of Daniel backslide just before rapture takes Daniel out of the earth?

That can make sense and can easily fit into the pre- or mid-tribulation doctrine. However, the problem with this assumption is that it is not stated anywhere in the book of Daniel or anywhere in the entire Bible that the three guys backslide. In fact, Chapter 2 of the book of Daniel ends with the fact that God promotes the four—Daniel, Shadrack, Meshach and Abednego—above the magicians who worship idols, for their uprightness. And there is no hint in the third chapter that the three stop serving God. On the contrary, the hint given in Chapter 3 is that the three still continue to serve God. Let us look at it in Daniel 3:16–17:

> *16. Shadrach, Meshach, and Abednego, answered and said to the king, O Nebuchadnezzar, we are not careful to answer thee in this matter. 17. If it be so, our God **whom we serve** is able to deliver us from the burning fiery furnace, and he will deliver us out of thine hand, O king.*

Notice the above passage. The way the three guys respond to Nebuchadnezzar's anger gives an idea of what has transpired, before the event. They say to an angry, proud, authoritarian king that the God whom they serve . . . to me, this means that there has been no broken service to the God they are talking about, neither are they new to Him. It seems to me that the passage is pointing out a continuous service to a God they have come to know with experience. Listen to the tone of their voice. It doesn't sound like unserious Christians who are afraid

99

for their lives. It sounds like people who have enjoyed the power of God's saving grace and are willing to sacrifice their lives even when the God they trust, in His infinite sovereignty, decides not to save them.

Another issue with the doctrine is that, in the story, at the end of it all, Christ shows up for them. They come out of the fire untouched. A decree is made that reverence be given to the God of Shadrack, Meshach, and Abednego. But in the time of the antichrist, it will not have such a happy ending, at least in the physical realm and at the moment of the reign of the antichrist. The three and a half years of great tribulation will be a time given to the antichrist to wreak great havoc on the earth. Until his time is up, he will continue to wreak havoc on anyone or anything that opposes him. But until then, he will do as he wills, and nothing and nobody can get in his way. Look at how Daniel puts it in Daniel 11:36:

> *36. And the king shall do according to his will; and he shall exalt himself, and magnify himself above every god, and shall speak marvellous things against the God of gods, and shall prosper till the indignation be accomplished: for that that is determined shall be done.*

That passage is speaking about the antichrist. It says he shall do according to his will and no one can stop him. That is a little different from what happens in the story of Daniel 3. Although Nebuchadnezzar is a dictator, he cannot destroy the three Hebrew men because God intervenes. This passage also says he will say marvelous things against God. It means he will blaspheme against the most high without immediate repercussion. Look at how John relates the same event in Revelation 13:5–6:

> *5. And there was given unto him a mouth speaking great things and blasphemies; and power was given unto him to continue forty and two months. 6. And he opened his mouth in blasphemy against God, to blaspheme his name, and his tabernacle, and them that dwell in heaven.*

Did you notice that what is related in Revelation 13 is more or less the same as what is related in Daniel 11? Both passages are speaking about the same person. Did you also notice that in Revelation, it says power is given unto the antichrist to do as he wills? It is not so with Nebuchadnezzar, according to the doctrine of Daniel 3. In the case of Daniel 3, Nebuchadnezzar bows to God and forces everyone under his domain to revere the God of all gods. Look at it in Daniel 3:28–29:

> *28. Then Nebuchadnezzar spake, and said, Blessed be the God of Shadrach, Meshach, and Abednego, who hath sent his angel, and delivered his servants that trusted in him, and have changed the king's word, and*

yielded their bodies, that they might not serve nor worship any god, except their own God. 29. Therefore I make a decree, That every people, nation, and language, which speak any thing amiss against the God of Shadrach, Meshach, and Abednego, shall be cut in pieces, and their houses shall be made a dunghill: because there is no other God that can deliver after this sort.

Can you see that? He not only worships God but also makes it a decree for every nation and people under his reign to do the same. That is completely contrary to what the antichrist will do. The antichrist will not worship God, neither will he tell the whole world to revere the true God like Nebuchadnezzar does in the passages we examined. On the contrary, he will blaspheme all through his reign and put himself in the place of God until Christ comes and destroy him. There is therefore no basis of comparison between this story and rapture.

Now, let us assume that the doctrine is centered on Daniel's disappearance alone, ignoring the other parts of the story. Hence, the doctrine will sound like this: Just as Daniel is not there when Nebuchadnezzar unleashes tribulation on those who do not worship his image, so shall the church be taken out of the earth just before the great tribulation. That sounds better. But it also has a problem. The problem with that is that the inference is made by someone other than the Bible itself. The Bible is the best interpreter of itself. When the days of Lot are to be compared to an event in the end time, the Bible picks the particular event in the days of Lot and also picks a specific event in the last days to compare it with. Let's look at that example again in Luke 17:28–30:

> *28. Likewise also as it was in the days of Lot; they did eat, they drank, they bought, they sold, they planted, they builded; 29. But the same day that Lot went out of Sodom it rained fire and brimstone from heaven, and destroyed them all. 30. Even thus shall it be in the day when the Son of man is revealed.*

Did you notice how Jesus puts it in the above verses? A specific event in the days of Lot is compared to a specific event in the end time. There is also another example where such a comparison is made. A specific event in the days of Noah is compared to a specific event in the end time. See how that matter is related in Matthew 24:37–39:

> *37. But as the days of Noe were, so shall also the coming of the Son of man be. 38. For as in the days that were before the flood they were eating and drinking, marrying and giving in marriage, until the day that Noe entered into the ark, 39. And knew not until the flood came, and took them all away; so shall also the coming of the Son of man be.*

Can you see that in the above passage? Now then, the New Testament is filled with passages drawing inferences from the Old Testament. Almost every book in the New Testament has at least one reference from the Old Testament. Let us give a few examples here. We already gave examples from two books in the four Gospels. The other two of the Gospels not mentioned also have several references from the Old Testament. But let's look at examples from other books of the New Testament. Act 2:16–17

> *16. But this is that which was spoken by the prophet Joel; 17. And it shall come to pass in the last days, saith God, I will pour out of my Spirit upon all flesh: and your sons and your daughters shall prophesy, and your young men shall see visions, and your old men shall dream dreams:*

This is an account of Peter's first sermon immediately after the Baptism of the Holy Ghost. In that sermon, he references Joel 2:28 and compares it to what the visitors to Jerusalem at Pentecost are seeing. Notice how he puts it—this is that. What is that? Meaning what the visitors are observing at that time is exactly what Joel says. Can you see that? He compares a specific event in the past to a specific event in the present. Look at another example in the letter of Paul to the Corinthians: 2 Corinthians 3:13:

> *13. And not as Moses, which put a vail over his face,*

104

that the children of Israel could not stedfastly look to the end of that which is abolished

In this example, Paul is referencing Exodus 34:33. And he is using a specific event that took place in the past to explain a specific situation in the present and future. We can go on and on. Almost every book in the New Testament has at least one of such references from the Old Testament. From the hundreds of references of the Old Testament in the New Testament, NONE of it mentions anything close to the doctrine that says Daniel is missing from the tribulation of the fiery furnace because it is an allegory of how the church will be saved from the coming tribulation. Should we not wonder that as important as this issue is, there is no single mention of that in the New Testament (not even close)? It is therefore a dangerous thing to do, making the Bible say what it is not saying. There are hundreds (if not thousands) of passages, both in the New and Old Testament, that explicitly tell us what to expect concerning ALL aspects of the matters of the end time that heaven expects us to know. It will be a dangerous act to create additional facts to add to the already existing thousands of truths concerning the topic. Whatever is created by humans will definitely mislead and can even have eternal consequences.

Now then, someone may ask, are you telling me there is no single reference of Daniel in the New Testament? The answer is no. Let us look at some passages in the New Testament that reference the book of Daniel: Matthew 24:15:

15. When ye therefore shall see the abomination of desolation, spoken of by Daniel the prophet, stand in the holy place, (whoso readeth, let him understand:)

Here, Jesus is quoting from the book of Daniel, and it is related to the matter we have been discussing—the matter of the end. Jesus is talking about the abomination of desolation that the antichrist will set up in the most holy place in the temple at Jerusalem during his seven-year reign as prophesied by Daniel. Let's look at the passage in the book of Daniel where Jesus quoted from. Daniel 9:27:

27. And he shall confirm the covenant with many for one week: and in the midst of the week he shall cause the sacrifice and the oblation to cease, and for the overspreading of abominations he shall make it desolate, even until the consummation, and that determined shall be poured upon the desolate.

Notice that this passage in Daniel only mentions the overspreading of abominations. Notice also that the abominations talked about happen in the middle of the week. Meaning in the middle of the seven-year reign of the antichrist. Let's look at a much clearer picture that Daniel paints about this same event that will take place during the reign of the antichrist. Daniel 11:31:

31. And arms shall stand on his part, and they shall

pollute the sanctuary of strength, and shall take away the daily sacrifice, and they shall place the abomination that maketh desolate.

Did you see that it is exactly what Jesus is talking about in Matthew 24:15? That is one of the references of the book of Daniel from the New Testament. Let's take a look at another. Mark 13:14:

14. But when ye shall see the abomination of desolation, spoken of by Daniel the prophet, standing where it ought not, (let him that readeth understand,) then let them that be in Judaea flee to the mountains:

Notice that this is almost exactly the same as what Matthew reports in Matthew 24:15. Mark is reporting the same exact sermon and also mentioning the quote Jesus made from the book of Daniel. Another place where the book of Daniel is quoted in the New Testament is in Hebrews 11:33:

33. Who through faith subdued kingdoms, wrought righteousness, obtained promises, stopped the mouths of lions,

Here, Paul is teaching about faith. He is talking about heroes of the Bible who through faith subdued the power of the enemy and brought to pass the purpose of God. Though the name of Daniel is not mentioned in that verse unlike in the subsequent verses, but he is quoting from Daniel 6:22:

> *22. My God hath sent his angel, **and hath shut the lions' mouths**, that they have not hurt me: forasmuch as before him innocency was found in me; and also before thee, O king, have I done no hurt.*

We have reviewed some New Testament passages that reference the book of Daniel. There are several more, but none of the passages mention Daniel being out of town when the other three are thrown into the fiery furnace as a picture of the rapture to come. This is therefore a dangerous way to infer from the Scriptures. Anyone can take any part of the Scriptures and make it say whatever he/she wants it to say. This is very misleading, especially in matters that the Bible takes over one-third of its pages explaining.

Genesis 5:24 doctrine:

> *24. And Enoch walked with God: and he was not; for God took him.*

The doctrine created from this passage is very simple. Just as Enoch was no more, so will the church be taken at rapture and will be no more. I guess the doctrine means that Enoch was taken before the wrath of God was poured out on humanity through the flood. The passage in Genesis 5:24 does not insinuate any such thing, neither does any verse in the entire Chapter 5 of the book of Genesis say that.

There are a few things wrong with that doctrine. First, Enoch's disappearance occurred at least six hundred years before the flood came. There is no way we can or should link his disappearance to being taken out of the earth in order to prevent him from experiencing the coming tribulation. The above passage doesn't state the way in which Enoch disappeared. It just says he was no more. The Bible still remains the best source of interpreting itself. There are other places in the Bible that specifically mention the exact thing that happened to Enoch. Let us look through the Bible to see if what happened to Enoch was rapture or something else. Let's start our search from Hebrews 11:5:

> *5. By faith Enoch was translated that he should not see death; and was not found, because God had translated him: for before his translation he had this testimony, that he pleased God.*

Did you notice the word used to describe Enoch's disappearance? Translation. What does that mean? It means to be transported or exchanged or to change sides. Again, notice that the reason for his translation is mentioned in the above passage. Did you notice that the passage doesn't mention anything near being translated in order to escape the coming tribulation? If there is any reason for his translation we can infer from the above passage, it is that it was because he pleased God. If the Bible doesn't say or mean that Enoch is a picture of the rapture of the church, then we stand in danger of stepping into error if we do. Again, the Bible uses the word "translation" here. It is different from the words "caught up," which are used to describe rapture. They are two different phenomena. The first is more like an easy ride, while the second is a forceful ride. It will therefore be out of place to infer that Enoch's translation can be taken to be an allegory of the rapture of the church.

There is also another passage in the New Testament where Enoch is mentioned in relation to the matters of the end. Jude 1:14–15:

> *14. And Enoch also, the seventh from Adam, prophesied of these, saying, Behold, the Lord cometh with ten thousands of his saints, 15. To execute judgment upon all, and to convince all that are ungodly among them of all their ungodly deeds which they have ungodly committed, and of all their hard speeches which ungodly sinners have spoken against him.*

Looking at the above passages carefully, we can see that it does not in any way infer or give the slightest hint that the translation of Enoch is a picture of the church at rapture. It only tells us that Enoch prophesied and tells us what he prophesied about. If there is anywhere the Bible should tell us that the translation of Enoch is a picture of the rapture of the church, this passage would have been a good place to mention that. But the passage doesn't say that. That probably means it is not heaven's intention for us to relate Enoch's translation to rapture.

The other passages that mention Enoch are completely irrelevant to the subject of discussion; for example, Luke 3:37 mentions Enoch but talks about him in relation to the genealogy of Jesus Christ

Hence, it is clear that the doctrine of Genesis 5:24 was not generated from the Scriptures. It was generated by the assumption of man. That is a very dangerous thing to do given the importance of the matter.

1 Thessalonian 4:17–18 doctrine:

> *17. Then we which are alive and remain shall be caught up together with them in the clouds, to meet the Lord in the air: and so shall we ever be with the Lord.*
> *18. Wherefore comfort one another with these words.*

Chapter 10

The doctrine around these Scriptures is that Verse 18 says comfort one another with these words. The words being referred to here are the words in Verse 17 that say we shall be caught up together with the dead in Christ to meet the Lord in the air. Hence, the doctrine concludes that rapture is a phenomenon that should be used to give comforting words to the believers that they will not go through the great tribulation.

If we are to give a summarized version of the doctrine, it says that the believers should comfort one another or be consoled because rapture will take them out of the earth just before the great tribulation starts. Is that really what Paul is trying to say? This is another doctrine built on a standalone verse, Verse 18. In order to avoid the danger of taking the passage out of context, let us consider it from the beginning of the conversation to see exactly what Paul is trying to say.

Chapter 4 of 1 Thessalonians (on which the doctrine is built), has two subjects of discussion. The first subject of discussion is from Verse 1 through Verse 12. The second subject of discussion starts from Verse 13 and ends at Verse 18. In the first subject of discussion, Paul is admonishing the Thessalonian Church on how to live a holy life before God. The second subject of discussion is completely different. If you have a Bible that assigns a topic to each section, you will notice that the second part is given a title just before Verse 13 starts. Now then, the introductory statement of the second subject of discussion gives us an idea of the topic of discussion. Let us look at it: 1

Thessalonians 4:13:

13. But I would not have you to be ignorant, brethren, concerning them which are asleep, that ye sorrow not, even as others which have no hope.

Look at the passage carefully as we try to take it piece by piece to see exactly what Paul is trying to communicate. A group of people in the Thessalonian Church are sorrowful because of the death of some very close family members. Can you see that in the above passage? " . . . concerning them which are asleep (dead), that ye sorrow not . . ." Hence, we can see from the introductory verse, Verse 13, that the subject of discussion is that Paul is trying to console those who have been sorrowing because of their family members who have died. It is possible that the members who have died were too young to die. This is usually what causes great sorrow. But then we cannot hold unto this supposition because the passage doesn't mention the age of those who have died. And more so, some people can still have great, inconsolable sorrow for loved ones even if they died after living a hundred years. Therefore, it is wrong to assume something when the Bible doesn't expressly say so. The rule I advocate is to keep silent where the Bible is silent and be loud where the Bible is loud. Never try to make the Bible say what it is not saying, for that is a very dangerous thing to do. Now then, we are clear on the subject of discussion of the second part of 1 Thessalonians 4—trying to bring comforting words to those who mourn their dead. The next thing we need to look for is how Paul hopes to bring comfort to them. What can he say that will make them stop sorrowing or stop mourning? It is possible that the mourning or sorrowing has been going on for too long. Again, we cannot say that is the situation because the Bible doesn't say that. Whatever the case is, Paul tries to comfort them with his letter to them. We now need to see how. Look at the next verse, 1 Thessalonians 4:14:

14. For if we believe that Jesus died and rose again, even so them also which sleep in Jesus will God bring with him.

Now, remember Verse 13 was saying to them not to sorrow like the world does, who have no hope? Verse 14 is now saying if we, as Christians, believe that Jesus rose from the dead, then we should also believe that our loved ones whom we mourn for, will one day rise from the dead. Is that not comforting for anyone mourning for a dead one whom he/she assume will never be seen again? Are we not still using those words to comfort those who mourn for the loss of their loved ones today? Let's continue. That's not all Paul says. This is just the beginning of the comforting words of Paul to the believers mourning their dead. Before we move to the next verse, let's do a quick recap of what has transpired from Verse 13 through Verse 14. Some Thessalonian Christians who are mourning their dead receive a letter from Paul telling them not to mourn or sorrow like the unbelievers do. And that one day, their loved ones will rise up just like Jesus rose from the dead. That is the summary so far. You will notice that I have not said anything that these two verses don't say. Now let's move to the next verse and see what brother Paul is trying to further say about the matter of comfort. 1 Thessalonians 4:15:

> *15. For this we say unto you by the word of the Lord, that we which are alive and remain unto the coming of the Lord shall not prevent them which are asleep.*

Notice the first word that introduces Verse 15: for. This means he is still going on or continuing with his words of encouragement or words of comfort to those who mourn. He started, in the previous verses we reviewed, by saying that as Christ rose from the dead to live again, so will the dead in Christ rise from the dead someday. Now in Verse 15 Paul is saying this resurrection of the dead will take place at the coming of the Lord. On that day, we who are alive will not prevent the dead in Christ from rising. Can you see that in Verse 15? Now let's move to Verse 16: 1 Thessalonians 4:16:

> *16. For the Lord himself shall descend from heaven with a shout, with the voice of the archangel, and with the trump of God: and the dead in Christ shall rise first:*

Now then, notice that this verse is further describing how the resurrection will happen at the coming of the Lord. Paul is saying here that the dead in Christ shall rise first at the second coming when the

Lord Himself will descend with a shout and with the voice of an archangel. Alright then, let's look at the next verse: 1 Thessalonians 4:17:

> *17. Then we which are alive and remain shall be caught up together with them in the clouds, to meet the Lord in the air: and so shall we ever be with the Lord.*

After the dead in Christ resurrect to meet with the Lord in the sky, then, we who are alive at His coming will be caught up or raptured with them. Then, he, Paul now concludes with Verse 18, the verse from which the doctrine we have been trying to look at was coined : 1 Thessalonians 4:18:

> *18. Wherefore comfort one another with these words.*

Can you now see the context in which Paul uses the words "comfort one another with these words"? Which words is he referring to? The words that someday, those who have lost loved ones will meet them again. Now then, bringing everything together for better understanding, let us look at what the Paul is trying to communicate versus what the doctrine is saying:

Now check out what 1 Thessalonians actually says compared to what the doctrine says: Paul says, starting from Verse 13 of 1 Thessalonians 4, those believers who have lost loved ones should stop mourning as unbelievers who have no hope, that in the same way that Christ rose from the dead will believers who died in Christ rise from the dead at the Lord's coming, and we who are alive will not be left behind. Hence, the believers who mourn should be comforted with these words that one day they will definitely see their loved ones who have passed away. But the doctrine says that because Paul mentions rapture in Verse 17, he is trying to tell believers that we should comfort each other with the words that rapture will prevent us from going through the great tribulation, for just before the great tribulation starts, we shall be caught up. That is the context of the "comfort one another with these words" part of the doctrine. Can you see that that is not what that passage is saying? From the analysis above, we can clearly say that someone is making the Bible say what it is not saying. Again, that is a very dangerous thing to do, especially given the level of importance of the subject of discussion.

Now then, let us look elsewhere in the Scripture to see if by "comfort," Paul is trying tell the Thessalonians that they should comfort themselves in the truth that they will not see the great tribulation or any tribulation for that matter or whether "comfort" is used by him for another purpose.

1 Corinthians 15:16–20:

> *16. For if the dead rise not, then is not Christ raised:*
> *17. And if Christ be not raised, your faith is vain; ye are yet in your sins. 18. Then they also which are fallen*

asleep in Christ are perished. 19. If in this life only we have hope in Christ, we are of all men most miserable. 20. But now is Christ risen from the dead, and become the firstfruits of them that slept.

Now look at the above passage. Here, Paul is trying to give the Corinthian Christians almost the same encouragement he has given the Thessalonian Christians. Notice the manner he uses in this particular discussion. Here, there are some preachers among the Corinthian Christians who are saying once someone dies, he/she is gone for good. No more resurrection of the dead. 1 Corinthians 15:12:

12. Now if Christ be preached that he rose from the dead, how say some among you that there is no resurrection of the dead?

This teaching leads to the same worry that the Thessalonian Christians had—our loved ones who have died are gone forever. Can you see how this kind of teaching can lead to that kind of thinking and eventually sorrow? Look at how Paul puts it in 1 Thessalonians 4:13–14:

13. But I would not have you to be ignorant, brethren, concerning them which are asleep, that ye sorrow not, even as others which have no hope. 14. For if we believe that Jesus died and rose again, even so them also which sleep in Jesus will God bring with him.

Can you now see that it is the exact same situation that has made Paul write to the Thessalonian Christians that also makes him write to the Corinthian Christians? Now if the doctrine holds water, Paul would have encouraged the Corinthians in the same exact way he has encouraged the Thessalonians by telling them not to worry that one day rapture will take them away from the coming tribulation. But that is not what Paul does here. Let us see how Paul addresses this same issue with the Corinthian Church: 1 Corinthians 15:16–20

> *16. For if the dead rise not, then is not Christ raised:*
> *17. And if Christ be not raised, your faith is vain; ye are yet in your sins. 18. Then they also which are fallen asleep in Christ are perished. 19. If in this life only we have hope in Christ, we are of all men most miserable.*
> *20. But now is Christ risen from the dead, and become the firstfruits of them that slept.*

Notice how Paul puts it. If it is true that anyone who dies doesn't have any hope of resurrecting, then we can also say that Christ was not raised from the dead. This also translates to the fact that our faith is in vain because our faith is hinged on the fact that Christ resurrected. Look at the passage above (1 Thessalonians 4:13–14). Can you see the similarity in the two? Now then, look at 1 Corinthians 15:18

> *18. Then they also which are fallen asleep in Christ are*

perished.

Paul continues his exaltation here by saying, now, if we don't believe that there is resurrection after death, then our loved ones who died as Christians are perished and we shall never see them. Look at Verse 20 of that same passage: 1 Corinthians 15:20:

> *20. But now is Christ risen from the dead, and become the firstfruits of them that slept.*

Here, Paul finally brings the issue to a reasonable conclusion by confirming once again to the Corinthian Church that Christ definitely rose from the dead. This he has already confirmed in Verses 3–8 of 1 Corinthians 15 that Christ didn't only rise from the dead but that the resurrected Christ was seen by over five hundred people, most of whom are still alive at the time he (Paul) is writing to the Corinthian church. Now then, let me ask you a good question here. If Paul, after assuring the Corinthian Church that because of the fact that Christ rose from the dead, their loved ones will also be seen again, concludes his epistle to the Corinthian Church by saying:

1 Thessalonian 4:18:

> *18. Wherefore comfort one another with these words.*

Will that be out of place or off the course? No, it won't be. It is exactly what the church needed at the time. They needed to know that since Christ rose from the dead, their loved ones would also rise from the dead. And that that automatically means that they will definitely see their loved ones again. That is a reason to tell them to comfort one another. Therefore, it is clear, putting these two passages (1 Thessalonians 4:15–18 and 1 Corinthians 15:16–20) together, that Paul is NOT saying they should comfort themselves with the fact that rapture will take them out of the earth before the great tribulation. Rather, Paul is telling them that they should comfort themselves with the fact that one day the dead in Christ will resurrect and they will see their loved ones who have died again.

Let us look at another passage for better clarification on the matter

2 Corinthians 1:3–4:

> *3. Blessed be God, even the Father of our Lord Jesus Christ, the Father of mercies, and the God of all comfort; 4. Who comforteth us in all our tribulation, that we may be able to comfort them which are in any trouble, by the comfort wherewith we ourselves are comforted of God.*

Look at this passage above. It is written by the same person who wrote 1 Thessalonians 4:17–18, from which the doctrine was formed. It says something that is the complete opposite of what the doctrine says. Notice that Verse 3 of 2 Corinthians ends with the God of all comforts. Meaning God can endlessly comfort us. Notice that Verse 4 gives the exact situation in which God can comfort us. It says

121

"Who comforts us IN ALL our tribulation." Did you notice that? What does that mean? He comforts us IN our tribulation, not before our tribulation. Meaning, while we are in tribulation is when He comforts us. It doesn't say His comfort will take us out before the tribulation starts. Something is not adding up here. The same person, Apostle Paul, writes to the Corinthians that they should not worry, that in their trouble, God will comfort them, but writes to the Thessalonians that they will face no trouble for God will comfort them by taking them out before trouble starts. Something is not adding up. Either he is lying to one of the two or we have misinterpreted one of the two.

Let's do some further investigation. Let's look at Verse 7 of that same letter to the Corinthians (2 Corinthians 1:7):

> 7. *And our hope of you is stedfast, knowing, that as ye are partakers of the sufferings, so shall ye be also of the consolation.*

Did you notice the second part of that verse? "As you are partakers of the suffering." What could that mean? It means if you partake in the suffering with Christ in the form of persecution or tribulation, you will also partake in the consolation of Christ. It also means that there is no consolation or comfort without suffering. In other words, consolation comes after suffering, not before. But you look at it "commonsensically," does it make sense comforting someone who has not lost anybody or who has not been through

122

anything? Someone can say, "Oh no, it is comforting if you tell someone they won't have to go through any trouble." My question to this person will be, is "comforting" the right word to use in that situation?

Chapter 11

The Revelation 19 Doctrine

The Seven-Year marriage supper of the Lamb

This is another doctrine around the great tribulation. It states that while the antichrist is reigning on earth for seven years, the raptured Christians will be in heaven with Christ, observing the marriage supper of the Lamb. This passage is also used to justify the pre-tribulation rapture doctrine. It is said that while the antichrist is reigning for seven years on earth, the raptured church (which was taken shortly before the antichrist was revealed to the world) will be in heaven celebrating the marriage supper of the Lamb, which will also last for the same time period the antichrist reign (seven years). This, to me, is a very important event that Christians and heaven should look forward to. The marriage supper of the Lamb is more or less the wedding reception (wedding feast) of Christ. There should be nothing as important as that ceremony. Christ has waited for His bride, the church, for over two thousand years. Now the Bride is finally in heaven, the wedding has been conducted, and the reception after the wedding is supposed to last for seven years, according to the doctrine. As interesting as that doctrine is, there is no single passage in the Bible that tells us that this is going to happen. If the doctrine is true, I don't know of anything else that should have greater importance in the heart of Christ and/or Christians with regards to the end time. The day a man finally takes his long-awaited bride home is supposed to be a day of great importance in his life. But as important as that day is to Christ, the Bible is completely silent about its duration. Only one passage mentions the phrase "the marriage supper of the Lamb" (we shall consider that passage later on). This is very strange to me, given the importance of the matter. Is heaven trying to hide something that important from us or the world?

Now then, the Bible clearly tells in every way possible that the antichrist will be given seven years, which will be divided into two three-and-a-half-year periods. The Bible tells this duration in days, months, and in years so that we won't be confused about it and so that no man can say that one week means a thousand years or whatever meaning they want to read into it. Let us consider some of the passages: Daniel 9:27:

> *27. And **he** shall confirm the covenant with many for **one week**: and in the **midst of the week** he shall cause the sacrifice and the oblation to cease, and for the overspreading of abominations he shall make it desolate, even until the consummation, and that determined shall be poured upon the desolate.*

Notice how the Bible puts it in that passage. The "he" in that passage is referring to the antichrist. The one week in that passage is the last week of the seventy weeks that were spoken about earlier on in the passage (Daniel 9:24). We know that in the seventy-week prophecy, each day represent a year. Hence, the one week allotted to the antichrist is a seven-year period. Notice also, that the passage says in the middle of his reign, he shall become something else (that's when the great tribulation starts). That is the last three and a half years, which is the period of the great tribulation. This particular passage represents the antichrist's reign in years. Let's consider another passage: Daniel 7:25:

> *25. And **he** shall speak great words against the most High, and shall wear out the saints of the most High, and think to change times and laws: and they shall be given into his hand until **a time and times and the dividing of time**.*

The "he" in this particular passage is referring to the antichrist. Notice the time he is given to wear out the saints (the great tribulation). A time, and times (two times), and the dividing of time (half of a time). A time means one year, two times mean two years, and half a time means half of a year. Putting everything together gives us three and a half years, which is the duration of the great tribulation. This is also confirming what is said about the seven-year reign of the antichrist in the first passage we considered (Daniel 9:27) —just in case we are confused about the week representing seven years. Notice that in Daniel 9, the period is divided into two three-and-a-half year periods. In the first three and a half years, he will pose to be a good fellow and will suddenly become a monster in the last three and a half years. Daniel 7 does not mention the first part. Now then, we can see in the above two passages that the Bible tells us about the same time period in various ways so we cannot miss it. In the first instance, it talks about it in symbolic form, using week to represent years, and in the second instance, it is clearly stated in years. Now let's look at other examples: Revelation 13:5:

> *5. And there was given unto **him** a mouth speaking great things and blasphemies; and power was given unto him to continue **forty and two months**.*

The above passage is also referring to the period of reign of the antichrist. The "him" in that passage is the antichrist. Notice for how long power will be given unto him to continue: forty-two months. What is that in years? Three and a half years ($12 + 12 + 12 + 6 = 42$). This exactly coincides with the above two passages we have looked at. So, here, the Bible tells us the same time period in months even though it has told us in years and in "week." Now then, let's consider the last passage on this matter: Revelation 11:2–3:

> *2. But the court which is without the temple leave out, and measure it not; for it is given unto the Gentiles: and the holy city shall they tread under foot forty and two months. 3. And I will give power unto my two witnesses, and they shall prophesy a thousand two hundred and threescore days, clothed in sackcloth.*

Notice how John the revelator talks about the same time

127

period we have been looking at. He says a part of the temple in Jerusalem will be given to the gentiles (the antichrist and his army) for a period of forty-two months (which we have heard from Daniel). What is new here is the number of days that the two witnesses will be given power to prophesy. It should also be of note that while the antichrist is given the outer court of the temple, the two witnesses will be carrying out their ministry. Hence, the two events will be running concurrently. Now, notice how the duration of their ministry (which is also the time period the antichrist will exact his will on the people) is recorded—in days. Let's see if it adds up to all the other accounts we have looked at. The days put here is 1260. In the Jewish calendar (which is what is represented in Revelation), a year is 360 days. Hence, $360 + 360 + 360 + 180 = 1260$. Exactly three and a half years.

Now then, we have seen how the Bible represents the time period during which the antichrist will unleash his evil on earth. It is shown in days, months, and years. In every way possible, it seems heaven wants us to know that the three and a half years is literal. No hidden meaning to it. No Greek or Hebrew word or figure that represents something else. It is as clear as day.

Now then, back to the issue at hand—seven years of the marriage supper of the Lamb. Notice, so far, from all the passages we have looked at, that the Bible is not shy regarding the duration the antichrist will unleash his evil on earth. It is mentioned at least three times in both the Old and the New Testament in the all ways possible (days, months, and years). This is an event that supposedly, Christians

128

who read the Bible today will not be part of. The Bible utilizes a reasonable number of pages telling us about the number of years it will go on for. On the other hand, as regards the marriage supper of the Lamb, which is an event organized specifically for Christians, it is not mentioned anywhere in the Bible that it will last for seven years. Isn't that strange? Is God more interested in the antichrist than in His children? Does God want us to know about an event that we are supposedly not going to be part of at the expense of the main event in heaven that we are supposed to be the major players of? Why would God tell us about our reward in heaven and skip telling us about the marriage supper of the Lamb that we are supposed to be the main guests at? Something is not adding up here.

It is clear to me that God put all these information in the Scripture for us so that we can know about the coming events and walk in the light of the information we have gleaned. We know details about the seven-year reign of the antichrist based on what the Bible says about it. But there are no such details concerning an event that is supposed to be the climax of everything for believers. This suggest to me that there is no such event in the agenda of God. If there was, there would have been at least a mention.

Let us examine the passage where this doctrine is likely to come from: Revelation 19:6–9:

6. And I heard as it were the voice of a great multitude,

and as the voice of many waters, and as the voice of mighty thunderings, saying, Alleluia: for the Lord God omnipotent reigneth. 7. Let us be glad and rejoice, and give honour to him: for the marriage of the Lamb is come, and his wife hath made herself ready. 8. And to her was granted that she should be arrayed in fine linen, clean and white: for the fine linen is the righteousness of saints. 9. And he saith unto me, Write, Blessed are they which are called unto the marriage supper of the Lamb. And he saith unto me, These are the true sayings of God.

Notice what is said in Verse 7. It says the marriage of the Lamb has come. A great multitude in heaven are rejoicing and worshipping God because the marriage of the Lamb has come. Notice that as far as heaven is concerned, in this matter, the most important thing is that the wife has made herself ready. For if the wife had not made herself ready, the marriage would not have come. Hence, the rejoicing and the singing and the worship by the great multitude seen is basically because they can now witness the marriage of the Lamb, for the wife has made herself ready. Now look at Verse 8. The entire verse is dedicated to telling us how the wife made herself ready. First, she was given a fine clean and white linen (I suppose a wedding gown). Notice that after that, the author tells us how she got the gown. The gown is a symbol of the righteousness of the saints. The white linen came with a price. Let's look at a passage that talks about the price that brought about the white linen: Daniel 11:33–35:

> *33. And they that understand among the people shall instruct many: yet they shall fall by the sword, and by flame, by captivity, and by spoil, many days. 34. Now when they shall fall, they shall be holpen with a little help: but many shall cleave to them with flatteries. 35. And some of them of understanding shall fall, to try them, and to purge, and to make them white, even to the time of the end: because it is yet for a time appointed.*

Notice how that passage starts: Those with understanding. Understanding of what? Understanding of the times and the seasons in which they live. One would think that understanding should save one from calamity. But in the above passage, it seems that understanding brought them into calamity. Look at what those with understanding will suffer in Verse 33. They shall be killed (sword), they shall be burnt alive (flame), they shall be imprisoned (captivity), and they shall be abused (spoil) for many days. Not few, not some, but many days. What will this do to them? Look at Verse 35. All these things—sword, flame, captivity and spoil—are to try them and to purge them so that they can be white. Going back to Revelation 19, notice what is said about the wife in Verse 7. She has made herself ready. You see that? She is given the white linen because she paid the price. Little wonder there is great rejoicing for her. She went through a difficult time, but she came out as pure as gold. Just like impure gold is passed through fire to get refined and pure gold.

Now then, lets continue with our analysis on Revelation 19. Look at Verse 9:

> *9. And he saith unto me, Write, Blessed are they which are called unto the marriage supper of the Lamb. And he saith unto me, These are the true sayings of God.*

The passage above says blessed are those who are called to the marriage supper of the Lamb. That's all that is said about the marriage supper. Nowhere else in the Bible is it mentioned. It doesn't state anywhere that it will last for seven years. I am not sure where the idea came from, but I am sure it is not in the Bible. Someone might say, "Oh, the idea was gotten from the way Jewish people celebrate their wedding." In a Jewish wedding, the final phase of the wedding ceremony culminates in a great feast, the marriage supper, which can last for several days. But even that doesn't last for seven years. But someone might say, "Oh no, it usually lasts for seven days. Each day of the seven days is taken to be one year, and that is how they come about the seven years." The passage doesn't even mention how long the supper will last. Because not all Jewish weddings last for seven days. Some last for three days, and some last for more than seven days. Hence, if the Bible wanted us to take seven days for seven years, it would have at least mentioned how long the supper will last. The

Bible does that with an event that people think we shall not be part of, so why wouldn't it do the same with an event we are expected to be part of?

Now then, there is a parable of Jesus that talks about a certain king who arranged a marriage for His son in Matthew 22. Even that does not state that the supper will last for seven years. So, wherever that idea came from, it definitely was not from the Bible. Hence, such a doctrine should be approached with caution.

The Truth about rapture as the Bible Puts it

You will notice that so far, we have not taken any verse out of context to make it say what the Bible is not saying. We have looked at every doctrine out there that we can lay our hands on to see whether the doctrine is in line with what the Bible says. You can see for yourself what the Bible says versus what the doctrine says. We have so far allowed the Bible to do the talking while we did the listening. I am sure there are other Bible passages that people are laying claim on as regards pre-tribulation and mid-tribulation rapture, but I am not yet familiar with them. In this next phase, we shall continue in that line—allowing the Bible to speak for itself without inference or making the Bible say what we want to hear. We shall explore what the Bible actually says about rapture (the Bible definitely has one or two things to say about the event). There will be no inferences and no original Greek meaning or Hebrew meaning that will throw anybody off or confuse anyone, and no allegory or mysterious revelation will be used. Nothing like the translators did this or that or according to eschatology or the episcopal this or that. We are just going to simply stick to the Bible and hear what it has to say on the subject. It will be exactly what the Bible is saying.

Chapter 12

The Thessalonians 2:1–4 truth:

> *1. Now we beseech you, brethren, by the coming of our Lord Jesus Christ, and by our gathering together unto him, 2. That ye be not soon shaken in mind, or be troubled, neither by spirit, nor by word, nor by letter as from us, as that the day of Christ is at hand. 3. Let no man deceive you by any means: for that day shall not come, except there come a falling away first, and that man of sin be revealed, the son of perdition;*

Before we look at this passage, let's give here a background story for better understanding. In His missionary journey, Paul went to Macedonia by the leading of the Holy Ghost through a vision he saw: Act 16:9:

> *9. And a vision appeared to Paul in the night; There stood a man of Macedonia, and prayed him, saying, Come over into Macedonia, and help.*

After this vision, Paul, perceiving that the Holy Ghost was telling him to continue his mission work in Macedonia, immediately took his team and went into Macedonia. After many days of ministry work, he and his team got into trouble again and were put in prison because they cast a demon out of a slave girl: Act 16:23:

16. And when they had laid many stripes upon them, they cast them into prison, charging the jailor to keep them safely.

They eventually set them free when they discovered they were Roman citizens. Then, Paul and his team continued on their journey, passing through Amphipolis and Apollonia and going on to Thessalonica: Act 17:1

1. Now when they had passed through Amphipolis and Apollonia, they came to Thessalonica, where was a synagogue of the Jews.

They stayed in Thessalonica for three weeks and taught the people there about Jesus being the Christ. They also taught them about the second coming of Christ and the antichrist. In those three weeks, Paul taught them all they needed to know about the second coming and the great tribulation: 1 Thessalonians 2:5:

5. Remember ye not, that, when I was yet with you, I told you these things?

Many Greeks and Jews were converted at this mission, and they formed the church in Thessalonica. After three weeks, Paul moved on to Berea after the Jews in Thessalonica stirred up trouble. After some time, Paul decided to write a letter to the church in

Thessalonica to follow up on them since he had not been able to visit them: 1 Thessalonians 2:18:

> *18. Wherefore we would have come unto you, even I Paul, once and again; but Satan hindered us.*

In that same letter, he encouraged them and reminded those that mourned for their lost ones to take comfort in the fact that one day the dead in Christ will rise and they will get to see their loved ones again.

The church wrote back to Paul, telling him that some fellows came to preach to them that rapture has already taken place. This translates to, "You said we shall see our loved ones again, but now rapture has come and gone, and none of them were resurrected." Then Paul wrote a second letter to them dispelling the lies that rapture had taken place. That brings us to 2 Thessalonians 2:1–3:

> *1. Now we beseech you, brethren, by the coming of our Lord Jesus Christ, and by our gathering together unto him, 2. That ye be not soon shaken in mind, or be troubled, neither by spirit, nor by word, nor by letter as from us, as that the day of Christ is at hand. 3. Let no man deceive you by any means: for that day shall not come, except there come a falling away first, and that man of sin be revealed, the son of perdition;*

137

Now then, let's look at what Paul was trying to communicate to the church about the matter of rapture. Note what Paul says in Verse 1: I plead with you, the church, concerning the matter of the coming of the Lord ... What is that? Now then, also note the phrase that follows: and by our gathering together unto Him ... What could that be? That is definitely rapture. At rapture, the believers will be gathered together to meet the Lord in the sky. Look at the description in 1 Thessalonian 4:16:

> *16. Then we which are alive and remain shall be caught up together with them in the clouds, to meet the Lord in the air: and so shall we ever be with the Lord.*

Can you see how that explains our gathering together unto Him? It means the same as "caught up together with Him." Look at another example in Matthew 24:31:

> *31. And he shall send his angels with a great sound of a trumpet, and they shall gather together his elect from the four winds, from one end of heaven to the other.*

Now then, it is clear from the above two passages that what Paul meant when he said: our gathering together unto Him is rapture. Now then, let us continue with Verse 2 of 2 Thessalonian 2:

> *2. That ye be not soon shaken in mind, or be troubled, neither by spirit, nor by word, nor by*

letter as from us, as that the day of Christ is at hand.

Note Verse 2. Paul is saying here that they should not be troubled by anything concerning that day, even if it is a spirit or word from anyone or even letter from himself, Paul, concerning the day. Look at Verse 3:

> *3. Let no man deceive you by any means: for that day **shall not come**, **except** there come a falling away first, and that man of sin be revealed, the son of perdition;*

This is the part that hits the nail on the head. Paul continues his admonition by telling them that they should not allow anyone to deceive them concerning that day or the event. Look at what follows: that day shall not come, except . . . What could that mean? It means rapture will not happen unless certain things happen first. What could these things be? Let's go on. Notice what comes after the word except: there be a falling away . . . Hence, a falling away must happen before rapture takes place. (We don't want to take time to explain the meaning of the phrase "falling away" because it is not within the scope of this book.) Now then, that's not all that comes after the word "except." Notice also that after the falling away, there is "and," meaning the falling away and the next phrase are the two things that MUST happen before rapture takes place. What is that other thing that must happen before rapture takes place? "That man of sin be revealed, the son of perdition." Who is the man of sin? Who is the son of perdition? That is the antichrist. Hence, putting everything together, Paul is telling the church that we should not be troubled in mind and not allow anyone to deceive us by any means concerning the day of rapture and that rapture WILL not COME until (or **except**) there is a falling away and the antichrist (the man of sin) is revealed. This is simply what Paul is saying. Notice that I just simply said what the Bible says without adding anything or trying to make it say what I want it to say.

Now then, someone might say, "Oh no, you got it all mixed up. The second coming is different from rapture. That passage is talking about the second coming and not rapture, so it makes sense for the antichrist to be here before the second coming." Alright, let's look at the passage again and determine whether it is talking about the second coming or rapture. But first, let me define the terms by the people who believe in pre-tribulation and mid-tribulation rapture. (this is not my definition or the Bible's definition of these terms):

According to them, the rapture of the church is when Jesus comes for the church and the second coming is when Jesus comes with the church. Now let us look at this definition in the light of the passage and see which of the two Paul is talking about.

2   Thessalonians 2:1–3:

1, Now we beseech you, brethren, by the coming of our Lord Jesus Christ, and by our gathering together unto him, 2. That ye be not soon shaken in mind, or be troubled, neither by spirit, nor by word, nor by letter as from us, as that the day of Christ is at hand. 3. Let no man deceive you by any means: for that day shall not come, except there come a falling away first, and that man of sin be revealed, the son of perdition.

Notice that Verse 1 clarifies the day Paul is talking about. He mentions two things there: by the coming of our Lord, and by our gathering together unto Him. Did you notice those two phrases in Verse 1 of the passage? What does "our gathering together unto Him" sound like? Does it sound like Christ coming for His church or like Christ coming with His church? If it is coming with His Church, why does he use the phrase "gathering together unto Him?" We only gather together unto Him at rapture. "**Coming for** His church" is when He appears in the sky, and we gather together to meet Him in the sky. Hence, it is clear that what Paul is referring to here is the rapture. Notice that there is the word "and" between the first phrase (by the coming of the Lord) and the second phrase (our gathering together unto Him). This suggests to me that Paul is referring to those two events happening on the same day. Notice what he says at the tail end of Verse 2: "that day of the Lord," not those days of the Lord. Hence, in describing the events that will occur at rapture, Paul says, first, there will be the coming of the Lord (in the sky) and the gathering together of the saints to meet Him in the sky. This is not different from how rapture is described in other passages: 1 Thessalonians 4:16–17:

> *16. For **the Lord himself shall descend from heaven with a shout, with the voice of the archangel, and with the trump of God: and the dead in Christ shall rise first: 17. Then we which are alive and remain shall be caught up together with them in the clouds,** to meet the Lord in the air: and so shall we ever be with the Lord.*

There is no doubt in the heart of any Christian that the above passage speaks of rapture. Now let's compare it to what Paul says in 2 Thessalonians 2 and determine whether it is actually the same. Look at the two phrases Paul uses to describe rapture in 2 Thessalonian 2 right in the above passages. Let's look at them together: *For the Lord Himself shall descend from heaven . . .* is exactly the same as *by the coming of our Lord Jesus Christ* and *then we which are alive and remain shall be caught up together with Him* is exactly the same as *by our gathering together unto Him.* Can you see the similarities?

Therefore, we can clearly see what the Bible is saying here. I clearly says that the event called rapture WILL NOT happen unles. two other events happen. What are those two other events? The fallin

142

away and the revealing of the antichrist to the world. This tells us that at least we shall still be here when the antichrist is revealed. What is not clear from the above passage is whether we shall be here throughout the seven-year reign of the antichrist or not.

Chapter 13

The Matthew 24 Truth

A man of God said, in one of his teachings, that Matthew 24 is the backbone of end time prophecies, and I perfectly agree with him. Matthew 24 is the only place where the events of the end time are chronologically stated. And it was given by our Lord Jesus Himself. So, it will be a good place to look at if we need to know the time allotted to rapture in the end time events. Let's do our best to look at it step-by-step and see what Jesus is telling the church. Matthew 24:1–2:

> *1, And Jesus went out, and departed from the temple: and his disciples came to him for to shew him the buildings of the temple. 2. And Jesus said unto them, See ye not all these things? verily I say unto you, There shall not be left here one stone upon another, that shall not be thrown down.*

Jesus has been teaching in the Temple and debating with the Pharisees, the Herodians, and the Sadducees. After the message and the debates, Jesus goes out of the Temple with His disciples to go to the Mount of Olives so as to rest. While ascending the slope of the mount of Olives, the team is positioned in such a way that they can easily see the beauty of the temple with its dazzling white marble. Notice what happens in Verse 1. The disciples point out the beauty of the Temple to Jesus: Matthew 24:1:

1, And Jesus went out, and departed from the temple: and his disciples came to him for to shew him the buildings of the temple.

Can you see that? Now then, Jesus responds to them in Verse 2. Let's look at it: Matthew 24:2:

2. And Jesus said unto them, See ye not all these things? verily I say unto you, There shall not be left here one stone upon another, that shall not be thrown down.

Jesus gives them the shock of their lives. The Temple will be so destroyed that no stone will be left on another. This is shocking to them. They say nothing at that moment. They try to think about what Jesus has said, but it seems like an impossible event. They continue in their ascent to the mount of Olives. When they get there, they settle down and sit comfortably. Then, the disciples decide to satisfy their curiosity and ask Jesus a further question on the issue. Matthew 24:3:

3. And as he sat upon the mount of Olives, the disciples came unto him privately, saying, Tell us, when shall these things be? and what shall be the sign of thy coming, and of the end of the world?

Notice the questions they ask Jesus. First, they say, "When

shall these things be?" What things? Remember the conversation they had in Verses 1 and 2? Jesus blew their minds by saying the Temple will be completely destroyed. The first question they ask Him is referring to the destruction of the Temple: "When shall these things be?" Notice they don't stop there. They ask another question: "What shall be the sign of your coming?" What exactly does that mean? It means what are the things we need to see in the event of the world that will give us a clue that your appearing is near, which also signify when the saints will be gathered unto Him? What is the sign to look for to know when your second coming will be? Now, there is a third question. What is it? And of the end of the world? What is that? Meaning, what is the sign we need to look for that will show the world is coming to an end? So here, they are asking two major questions that relate to our topic of discussion. First is: the sign of your appearing which, as we know, will usher in rapture, and, second, the sign of the end of the world, which many call the second coming. This will usher in the pouring out of the wrath of God upon the unbelievers. If Jesus answers the questions, then we should expect to have, in these passages, the full answer to everything concerning the matter of rapture and the wrath of God. These are clear and direct questions. Tel us the sign to look out for to know that your second coming and the end of the world is here. Let us see whether Jesus answers the questions or not. Matthew 24:4:

4. And Jesus answered and said unto them, Take heed that no man deceive you.

146

Notice the first three words in the verse above: "And Jesus answered." What does that mean? It simply means Jesus answered the questions. I have heard someone said no one knows anything about the second coming and the end of the world, and that Christ doesn't want us to know much about it. If that is true, then Jesus wouldn't have answered the questions unless, of course Jesus was deceiving the disciples. Somebody might say, "Oh no, Jesus didn't really want to refuse the disciples, but He needed to refuse in such a loving manner that the disciples will not get offended." Then I say you are either calling Jesus a liar or a deceiver. Because according to that thinking, you are saying Jesus didn't really want to answer the question but in order not to make them feel bad, He just said some things to get them off His back. So, let's search the Scriptures to see whether there is anywhere in the New Testament where it is mentioned that Jesus refused to answer the question of the disciples: Act 1:6:

> *6. When they therefore were come together, they asked of him, saying, Lord, wilt thou at this time restore again the kingdom to Israel?*

This is another scenario where the disciples ask another very important question. "Will you restore the kingdom back to Israel?" This is a clear question that demands a straightforward answer. What is the response of Jesus? Look at what Jesus says in the next verse: Act 1:7:

> *7. And he said unto them, It is not for you to know the*

147

*times or the seasons, which the Father hath put in his
own power.*

Did you notice what Jesus says in this verse? He clearly
doesn't answer the question. The verse doesn't start with "And he
answered." The verse starts with "And He said unto them." Did you
notice that? He goes on to say they don't need to know the time. He
gives them no clue at all. Unlike Matthew 24:4; He answers and says . .
. .

Therefore, we can say that Jesus expects us to know the signs
of His coming and the signs of the end of age because He doesn't
hesitate to answer the question. Now let's go through the chapter to
see if He talks about the timing of rapture, like Paul does; Matthew
24:4:

*4. And Jesus answered and said unto them, Take
heed that no man deceive you*

Notice the first thing Jesus says when He is answering the
question: Take heed that no man deceives you. Remember that this is
in line with what Paul said in 2 Thessalonians 2:3A:

3a. Let no man deceive you by any means

What it means to me is that concerning this matter called

rapture and the end time, men will deceive us. We can already see what Jesus and Paul say in the Bible in our world. Many say rapture will occur before the antichrist comes to the scene, many others say the event will happen three and a half years after the antichrist is revealed (mid-tribulation), and still others say it will occur after the tribulation. Can you already see that there is deception concerning the matter? Did you also notice that they don't say an angel will deceive us? They both mention man. And we can see that all these doctrines about rapture that have been flying around were created by men. I believe that the devil is at the root of it all. His major aim is to prevent us from God's best. The main purpose of the deception is to leave us unprepared or ill-prepared. Someone may say, "Oh, it doesn't matter. Whenever rapture comes, as long as we are believers, we shall go." The question I ask is do you think the devil deceives for fun? No!!! His deception is always targeted towards one goal—taking you away from the will and purpose of God for your life, which will ultimately lead to your destruction. Look at John 10:10A:

> *10. The thief cometh not, but for to steal, and to kill, and to destroy:*

His goal is not just to deceive us about the timing of rapture, it is ultimately to destroy us. What this means to me is that it is extremely important to know the timing the Bible assigns to the rapture, so we don't fall into the trap of the enemy. Hence, we can understand why Jesus's first warning is be careful not to be deceived.

And we also saw that Paul, about twenty years after the warning of Jesus to us, conveys the same exact warning concerning the timing of rapture.

Alright, let's go on with the search for the truth about rapture in Matthew 24. If we have to analyze what Jesus says verse by verse, we shall go beyond the scope of this book. We just want to see what the Bible says concerning the right timing of rapture.

Now then, Jesus continues in Verse 5; Matthew 24:5:

> *5. For many shall come in my name, saying, I am Christ; and shall deceive many.*

Notice the first word in that verse: "For." It means He is trying to link what He says in Verse 4 to Verse 5: Do not be deceived by any for . . . Can you see that? Let's move to the next verse, Verse 6. Matthew 24:6:

> *6. And ye shall hear of wars and rumours of wars: see that ye be not troubled: for all these things must come to pass, but the end is not yet.*

Notice the first word in that verse also. It starts with "And." I is clear what Jesus is doing. Giving us a sequence of events. Firs beware of deception from men. Then many shall come to say they ar Christ. The next thing is wars and rumors of war. He continues in thi

150

pattern, listing the events sequentially as they will happen. Read through yourself and you will see that each verse is linked alternatively to the other with "and" and "for." Now then, if you look at Verse 14, the dynamics sort of change a bit. Let's look at it together: Matthew 24:14:

> *14. And this gospel of the kingdom shall be preached in all the world for a witness unto all nations; and then shall the end come.*

Here, Jesus is saying that when the Gospel of the kingdom is preached in all the world, then shall the end come. This is profound. Jesus tells us a major sign to look for in order to know when the end will come. For those that are saying rapture can happen anytime from now, you notice that that is not what Jesus is saying here. We still have a reasonable part of the earth that doesn't have any knowledge of Christ or the Gospel. In fact, there are still some people that have never heard about Jesus. Until the message of the kingdom is preached to all nations, the end will not come. The word "nations" comes from a Greek word that means tribe. Now then, notice that before Verse 14, which speaks of the end, nothing is mentioned about rapture. You will also notice that from Verse 4 down to Verse 14, Jesus gives a chronological order of events of the end time. Let us run through the events without putting it in verses and see how it looks:

Be careful that no man deceives you about the matter of rapture because many shall come in my name saying I am Christ and they will deceive many. **And** you will hear of wars and rumors of wars; make sure that you are not troubled about that because all these things must happen (come to pass), but the end is not yet near. **For** nation shall rise against nation, and kingdom against kingdom, and there shall be famines (both of natural food and the true word of God) and pestilences (pandemics) and earthquakes in different places. All these are the beginning of sorrows. **Then** shall they deliver you up to be afflicted **and** shall kill you **and** you shall be hated of all nations for my name's sake. **And** then shall many be offended and shall betray one another and shall hate one another. **And** many false prophets shall rise and shall deceive many. **And** because sin shall abound, the love of many Christians shall wax cold. But he that shall endure unto the end shall be saved.

That is how it reads. Notice that no efforts have been made to make the Bible say what it is not saying. We've just written down what the Bible says using modern words instead of old words. For example, where the passage says "ye," it has been replaced with "you" (it is exactly the same meaning); where the passage says "take heed," it has been replaced with "be careful" (which also has the same meaning). Aside from that, we have just copied directly what Jesus says in Verses 4 through 13. Also notice that it is a chronological representation of events. How do I mean? Notice that after Jesus starts with "be careful," the next sentence starts with "and." Meaning the next follows after the first thing He says. In essence, after "many shall come saying they are Christ, you will begin to hear of wars and rumors of war." Also, notice the first word in the next sentence after that: "for." Meaning you will hear of wars and rumors of war because (for) nation will rise against nation and kingdom against kingdom. Can you see the chronological representation of the events? The next sentence starts with "then." Look at how everything sounds up until the word "then": Be careful not to be deceived by many who will say they are Christ and you will hear of wars and rumors of wars because nation shall rise against nation and kingdom against kingdom and there shall be famines and pandemics (pestilences) and earthquakes in different places. (While all these are going on), then they will deliver you up .. Can you see that it is clear Jesus is telling a story of the event as it will happen? Now then, you will also notice that Jesus didn't say anything about rapture before He talked about the end. From Verse 4 down to Verse 13, there is no mention of rapture. As far as we are concerned as Christians, rapture is a more important event than all that has been mentioned so far. There is no way Jesus would skip it because skipping it would amount to not answering the questions asked. Now let's continue with what Jesus says after Verse 14 to see whether He will tell us when the rapture will take place. Matthew 24:15:

15. When ye therefore shall see the abomination of desolation, spoken of by Daniel the prophet, stand in the holy place, (whoso readeth, let him understand:).

Notice how this verse starts. "When." Meaning Jesus is talking about time. If we have to put everything together from Verse 14 through to the beginning of Verse 15, then we have something like

153

this: This Gospel of the kingdom will be preached in all nations, then shall the end come. When you therefore see . . . What does that mean? It means while the preaching of the Gospel is going on, suddenly you shall see the abomination of desolation spoken of by Daniel set up in the holy place. Here, Jesus just told us that while the (final) Gospel is being preached to the whole world, then the antichrist will suddenly appear in the world scene (for he is the man that will set up the abomination of desolation in the holy place). We shall discuss that later on. But for now, let's focus on where we are going (when in the timeline did Jesus place rapture).

Before we point out where Jesus places rapture, notice so far, that what we have discovered from what Jesus has said so far (Mathew 24:4–15) has been consistent with what Paul says in 2 Thessalonians 2:2–7. Let us compare the two and see the similarities:

> *1. Now we beseech you, brethren, by the coming of our*
> *Lord Jesus Christ, and by our gathering together unto*
> *him, 2. That ye be not soon shaken in mind, or be*
> *troubled, neither by spirit, nor by word, nor by letter*
> *as from us, as that the day of Christ is at hand. 3. Let no*
> *man deceive you by any means: for that day shall no*
> *come, except there come a falling away first, and that*
> *man of sin be revealed, the son of perdition;*

Notice what Paul says in those verses. That day (Rapture) will not come EXCEPT there comes **a falling away** (backsliding or turning away from following Christ actively) and **the man of sin (the antichrist) be revealed**. Look at the passages we just examined in Matthew 24; Jesus says the exact same thing: Matthew 24:12–15:

> *12. And because iniquity shall abound, the love of many shall wax cold. 13. But he that shall endure unto the end, the same shall be saved. 14. And this gospel of the kingdom shall be preached in all the world for a witness unto all nations; and then shall the end come. 15. When ye therefore shall see the abomination of desolation, spoken of by Daniel the prophet, stand in the holy place, (whoso readeth, let him understand:)*

Notice what Jesus says in those verses of the Scripture: Because there will be lawlessness, many **Christians will backslide**, then there will be worldwide spread of the Gospel of the Kingdom. While that is going on, suddenly we shall hear that the **man of sin is revealed** who will desecrate the temple.

Can you notice the similarities in both passages? In the mouth of two or three witnesses, every word is established. But someone may say that Jesus doesn't mention rapture or the second coming in any of those verses. Exactly!! He doesn't mention rapture because those two things must first happen before rapture. That is the same exact way it is put in other passages that we shall also examine later.

The next logical question is where then does Jesus insert the matter of rapture that is of most importance to us Christians? Let us together examine where Jesus puts rapture.

Matthew 24:29–31:

> *29. Immediately after the tribulation of those days shall the sun be darkened, and the moon shall not give her light, and the stars shall fall from heaven, and the powers of the heavens shall be shaken: 30. And then shall appear the sign of the Son of man in heaven: and then shall all the tribes of the earth mourn, and they shall see the Son of man coming in the clouds of heaven with power and great glory. 31. And he shall send his angels with a great sound of a trumpet, and they shall gather together his elect from the four winds, from one end of heaven to the other.*

Now, before we begin to look critically at the above passages, let us remind ourselves why Jesus is saying everything He says right from Verse 4 through Verses 29, 30, and 31 (posted above). Jesus is trying to answer the three questions the disciples have asked Him. The questions are, Lord, please tell us, when shall the temple be destroyed, when shall the rapture be, and when shall the day of the Lord be? (Don't just take my word for it. Look at it yourself in Matthew 24:3) Jesus doesn't say He won't answer the questions. He clearly start answering the question from Verse 4 onwards. Therefore, we mus expect to see Him talk about rapture and the day of the Lord. Now let's go back to Matthew 24, from Verse 29. Notice how verse 29 starts: Immediately after the tribulation of those days ... Then jump to Verse 31. That verse starts with "and" —meaning it is continuing with whatever He is saying in Verse 29. Notice what He says in Verse 31. It says, Jesus shall send His angels with a great sound of trumpet. What does that sound like? Consider this passage: 1 Corinthians 15:52:

> *52. In a moment, in the twinkling of an eye, at the last trump: for the trumpet shall sound, and the dead shall be raised incorruptible, and we shall be changed.*

Comparing this verse in Corinthians to what Jesus says in Matthew 24:31, it is clear that both are referring to the same event—the Rapture. I believe without a shadow of doubt that Matthew 24:31 is referring to rapture, especially when you compare it to other passages that describe rapture. Again, let's do a second comparison so that the Scripture may be fulfilled—in the mouth of two or three witnesses, every word is established: 1 Thessalonians 4:16–17

> *16. For the Lord himself shall descend from heaven with a shout, with the voice of the archangel, and with the trump of God: and the dead in Christ shall rise first: 17. Then we which are alive and remain shall be caught up together with them in the clouds, to meet the Lord in the air: and so shall we ever be with the Lord.*

Notice how Paul describes the event (rapture) in this passage. For the Lord Himself will descend (Verse 16). Can you see that that is exactly what Jesus says in Matthew 24:30? Notice also that Verse 17 of the above passage is also saying the same thing with Matthew 24:31. Now, we can clearly say that what Jesus describes in Matthew 24:29–31 is rapture. The next logical question is, in the timeline of events as described by Jesus in Matthew 24, where does Jesus put rapture? He puts it after the great tribulation. What does that mean? It means we are going to be here while the antichrist reigns.

Someone might say, "Oh, you've got it all mixed up." The event that Jesus is describing in Verse 29 happens after tribulation and not the great tribulation. And that the great tribulation comes after the rapture that is mentioned in Verses 29 and 30. A good number of Christians believe this school of thought. Now let us look at these verses closely to see if this school of thought stands to reason. Matthew 24:29:

> *29. Immediately after the tribulation of those days*
> *shall the sun be darkened, and the moon shall not give*
> *her light, and the stars shall fall from heaven, and the*
> *powers of the heavens shall be shaken:*

Notice how the passage starts: "Immediately after THE tribulation of those days . . ." What could this mean? It means He is referring to a particular tribulation. Not just general tribulation. How then do we know the tribulation He is referring to? Could it be the one before the rapture or the one after the rapture? Let's check it out in Matthew 24:21:

> *21. For then shall be great tribulation, such as was not since the beginning of the world to this time, no, nor ever shall be.*

Can you see what Jesus is saying in Verse 21? He is clearly calling it the great tribulation. This should leave no doubt in the heart of anyone, that Jesus is talking about the great tribulation in this verse. And, from what Jesus is saying here, it is the only tribulation, one we have never seen the type of in the history of humanity. This is clearly speaking about the one and only great tribulation. Now then, look again at Verse 29. What Jesus says there now makes more sense:

> *29. Immediately after the tribulation of those days shall the sun be darkened, and the moon shall not give her light, and the stars shall fall from heaven, and the powers of the heavens shall be shaken:*

Immediately after **THE** tribulation of those days . . . Meaning Jesus is referring to the great tribulation talked about in Verse 21 because nowhere else in Mathew 24, from Verse 4 up until Verse 21, is any other tribulation mentioned. Neither is there anywhere else that tribulation is mentioned, from Verse 21 up until Verse 29. Hence, when Jesus says "after **THE** tribulation of those days," He is definitely referring to no other tribulation other than the one He talks about earlier (which is the only one He talks about before Verse 29).

Here, it is confirmed that rapture happens immediately after the great tribulation. Where then does Jesus place the regular tribulation Christians will suffer before the great tribulation? Look at Matthew 24:9:

> *9. Then shall they deliver you up to be afflicted, and shall kill you: and ye shall be hated of all nations for my name's sake.*

That is where the "regular" tribulation is placed. Right before the great fall away and right before the antichrist comes on the scene. And in fact, that tribulation is a tool God will use to weed out the tares from the wheat just before the end comes. This is to raise the called-out ones, Ekklesia, who will be anointed to preach the Gospel of the kingdom talked about in Matthew 24:14.

Notice that there is only one incidence of rapture mentioned in the whole of Matthew 24. No other rapture is mentioned. And the rapture that is mentioned comes immediately after the tribulation of those days. In summary, the timeline that Jesus gives in Mathew 24 is exactly the same as the one Paul mentions in 2 Thessalonians 2, only that Jesus goes a little further. Both Jesus and Paul say there will be a great fall away, and the antichrist will be revealed before rapture happens. Jesus goes further by inserting the great tribulation between the revealing of the antichrist and the rapture. Hence, from the two passages so far, we have the great fall away, the revealing of the antichrist, the great tribulation, and then rapture.

Chapter 14

The Daniel 7:19–27 truth:

Daniel is one of the prophets who extensively talked about the major kingdoms of the earth and the antichrist. Let us see what he has to say about rapture. Daniel 7:19–22:

> *19. Then I would know the truth of the fourth beast, which was diverse from all the others, exceeding dreadful, whose teeth were of iron, and his nails of brass; which devoured, brake in pieces, and stamped the residue with his feet; 20. And of the ten horns that were in his head, and of the other which came up, and before whom three fell; even of that horn that had eyes, and a mouth that spake very great things, whose look was more stout than his fellows. 21. I beheld, and the same horn made war with the saints, and prevailed against them; 22. Until the Ancient of days came, and judgment was given to the saints of the most High; and the time came that the saints possessed the kingdom.*

Before we look into the above passages, let us see the background story of the passage for better understanding. In the first year of Belshazzar, the king of Babylon, Daniel had a dream. This Belshazzar was the grandson of Nebuchadnezzar, and he was the last king of Babylon before it fell to the Medes and Persians. The dream was not clear to Daniel, so he approached an angel standing by to interpret the dream for him. The interpretation is what we see from Verse 19 through Verse 27. So let us look critically at what the dream means according to the interpretation given by the angel.

Here, we are mainly concerned with the fourth beast in the dream, which is the antichrist. Notice what is said about the beast in Verses 19 and 20:

> *19. Then I would know the truth of the fourth beast, which was diverse from all the others, exceeding dreadful, whose teeth were of iron, and his nails of brass; which devoured, brake in pieces, and stamped the residue with his feet; 20. And of the ten horns that were in his head, and of the other which came up, and before whom three fell; even of that horn that had eyes, and a mouth that spake very great things, whose look was more stout than his fellows.*

Here, the angel describes the kingdom of the fourth beast, which is the antichrist. The next logical question is how are we sure this fourth kingdom/beast in Daniel's dream is referring to the antichrist? It could have been anyone else in history past. How do we know for sure that this fourth beast is the antichrist and his kingdom?

Now notice the description given to this same beast in Verse 20 of Daniel Chapter 7: It has ten horns and three break. Out of the three that break comes a little horn, which is the antichrist. This little horn becomes the head of the government to whom the devil gives his authority. Notice these are the exact things said about the antichrist in Revelation 13:1–6:

> *1.And I stood upon the sand of the sea, and saw a beast rise up out of the sea, having seven heads and ten horns, and upon his horns ten crowns, and upon his heads the name of blasphemy. 2. And the beast which I saw was like unto a leopard, and his feet were as the feet of a bear, and his mouth as the mouth of a lion: and the dragon gave him his power, and his seat, and great authority. 3. And I saw one of his heads as it were wounded to death; and his deadly wound was healed: and all the world wondered after the beast. 4. And they worshipped the dragon which gave power unto the beast: and they worshipped the beast, saying, Who is like unto the beast? who is able to make war with him? 5. And there was given unto him a mouth speaking great things and blasphemies; and power was given unto him to continue forty and two months. 6. And he opened his mouth in blasphemy against God, to blaspheme his name, and his tabernacle, and them that dwell in heaven.*

Can you see how John puts it in the book of Revelation? These two books (Daniel and Revelation) were written hundreds of years apart but bear the same truth about the antichrist. Notice that in Daniel, the antichrist is described as a beast with ten horns, three of which break off to give way to a little horn. Notice how John describes the same beast in Revelation. It has seven heads and ten horns. Also notice that in Daniel, the little horn has eyes and a mouth that speaks great things. John tells us more about the great things this little horn speaks. Revelation 13:5:

> *5. And there was given unto him a mouth speaking great things and blasphemies; and power was given unto him to continue forty and two months. 6. And he opened his mouth in blasphemy against God, to blaspheme his name, and his tabernacle, and them that dwell in heaven.*

Can you see that? Now then, we are left without a doubt that the beast referred to in Daniel Chapter 7 is the antichrist. Someone might say, "But Daniel is referring to the kingdom and not the ruler of the kingdom." In prophecy relating to the end time, kingdom and kings are used interchangeably. The king represents the kingdom, and the kingdom usually takes the nature of the king. Hence, it is safe to say the fourth kingdom is actually referring to the fourth king, which is the antichrist. Let's consider an example from Daniel 2:32–33:

> *32. This image's head was of fine gold, his breast and*

his arms of silver, his belly and his thighs of brass, 33.
His legs of iron, his feet part of iron and part of clay.

This is the dream Nebuchadnezzar has in Daniel Chapter 2. The dream speaks of the major kingdoms that will appear on earth before Christ's second coming. Notice the interpretation Daniel gives to this in Verses 38 and 39:

> *38. And wheresoever the children of men dwell, the beasts of the field and the fowls of the heaven hath he given into thine hand, and hath made thee ruler over them all. Thou art this head of gold. 39. And after thee shall arise another kingdom inferior to thee, and another third kingdom of brass, which shall bear rule over all the earth.*

Notice what Daniel says concerning the first kingdom: You are this head of gold. What could this mean? It means the king cannot be separated from the kingdom. The king is the kingdom. Notice the next statement after that. After you shall arise another kingdom . . Can you see that? It is the same as saying, "After you shall arise another king . . ."

So going back to Daniel Chapter 7, the fourth kingdom being talked about is the fourth King, which is the antichrist. Now let's consider the rest of the verses: Daniel 7:21–22:

21. I beheld, and the same horn made war with the saints, and prevailed against them; 22. Until the Ancient of days came, and judgment was given to the saints of the most High; and the time came that the saints possessed the kingdom

Notice in Verse 21 how the antichrist makes war with the saint and prevailed. What does that mean? It is exactly what Jesus talks about in Matthew 24:21:

21. For then shall be great tribulation, such as was not since the beginning of the world to this time, no, nor ever shall be.

Notice that before Jesus talks about the great tribulation in Verse 21, He has already mentioned that the antichrist will be revealed to our world in Verse 15. The antichrist will unleash such a great tribulation on the saints (Christians) that only a few will survive. Notice also that in Daniel Chapter 7, the tribulation (war against Christians) continues until the Ancient of days come. Remember the first event Paul mentions when describing rapture in 2 Thessalonian 2? " . . . by the coming of our Lord." That is the only way Christians can be delivered from the terror of the antichrist—rapture. Notice that Jesus puts it the same exact way in Matthew 24:29–30:

29. Immediately after the tribulation of those days

*shall the sun be darkened, and the moon shall not give
her light, and the stars shall fall from heaven, and the
powers of the heavens shall be shaken: 30. And then
shall appear the sign of the Son of man in heaven: and
then shall all the tribes of the earth mourn, and they
shall see the Son of man coming in the clouds of
heaven with power and great glory.*

Notice how Jesus puts it here. Immediately after the great
tribulation, the elements start showing signs of the appearance of the
Ancient of days. The next verse says the Ancient of days appears in
His power and glory. The next thing that happens after the great
tribulation is the rapture, where Jesus comes to gather His saints out of
the tribulation. Therefore, we can say that Jesus, Daniel, and Paul are
in the same company. They all attest that the antichrist must first come
and unleash the great tribulation on Christians before rapture can
come. That's three witnesses so far. There are more witnesses. It
seems to me that God made great efforts to communicate this to us in
as many ways as possible.

Let's look at more example. Now then, in the same Chapter 7
of the book of Daniel, the event is expatiated on in Verses 23 through
28:

*23. Thus he said, The fourth beast shall be the fourth
kingdom upon earth, which shall be diverse from al*

kingdoms, and shall devour the whole earth, and shall tread it down, and break it in pieces. 24. And the ten horns out of this kingdom are ten kings that shall arise: and another shall rise after them; and he shall be diverse from the first, and he shall subdue three kings. 25. And he shall speak great words against the most High, and shall wear out the saints of the most High, and think to change times and laws: and they shall be given into his hand until a time and times and the dividing of time. 26. But the judgment shall sit, and they shall take away his dominion, to consume and to destroy it unto the end.

Did you notice what is being said about the antichrist in these verses? He shall wear out the saint. The words "wear out" are from a Hebrew word that means to afflict, to trouble, or to constantly harass. This is not different in meaning from tribulation (tribulation means to afflict). Hence, Daniel is telling us here that the saints will be subject to great distress (great tribulation) from the antichrist. Also notice that a time is put to how long the tribulation will last—three and a half years. Notice also that this will continue until judgment shall sit and his dominion shall be taken away. There is therefore a breaking point to the great tribulation, the coming of the Ancient of days as mentioned in the earlier verses we observed.

Hence, here, we have another Bible passage attesting to the

fact that rapture will not come unless the son of perdition—the antichrist—is revealed, and he (the antichrist) will wear out the saints in what we call the great tribulation. This is not different from what Jesus and Paul say. Only that, this goes a little further by telling us how long the tribulation will last. So, we have four witnesses attesting to the same sequence, one each from Jesus and Paul and two from Daniel.

Someone might say, "Oh no, you got it all mixed up. The saints referred to in these passages are the post-tribulation saints. These are the Christians who missed rapture." That means our third witness, Daniel, is being queried. We have to investigate the allegation so that we can be sure he is a viable witness to the other two witnesses (Jesus and Paul) because if the accusation is true, his speech will be opposite to what Jesus and Paul are saying.

First, if that doctrine is true, then it will mean that rapture is not mentioned in that passage. Is there any reason why Daniel would skip the rapture of the serious Christians and go straight on to talk about the antichrist and the unserious Christians? The next question one should ask is why are we Christians being informed about the matters of the end? I should guess the major reason we are being informed is to be aware when these things start happening so that we will know how to watch, pray, and prepare. If the saints mentioned in this passage are those left behind, then it should be of note that the entire event concerning the fourth kingdom mentioned in Daniel 7:19–27 take place after the assumed raptured event ("assumed" because the passages don't say any such thing). Then why are we being informed about what we will not be around to witness? What is the point?

Again, you will notice that after the Ancient of days comes to deliver the saints, judgment is passed and the kingdom is given to the saints. That's exactly how the passage puts it. Look at it here: Daniel 7:22:

> *22. Until the Ancient of days came, and judgment was given to the saints of the most High; and the time came that the saints possessed the kingdom.*

These are supposedly Christians who did not take their walk with God seriously before rapture. Suddenly, after rapture, at the most difficult time of humanity, they take their walk with God seriously and at the end of the world, they gain the kingdom and are to reign with Christ. The logical question to ask is where are the Christians who walked with God and were raptured? Should they not be more honored than those who failed Christ? Or better still, should they not at least receive the same honor as the saints who initially failed God? But Daniel never talks about them. Could it mean that they are not as important as those who initially failed God? Who should reign with Christ in the millennium? The people who took their walk seriously before rapture or those who, seeing rapture, decided to take God seriously? I think God is a fair judge and rewarder. If the saints that

171

missed rapture are honored with the kingdom, then the saints that made rapture should be honored with at least the same honor, if not greater. If not, why should any Christian prepare to make rapture, if they have no reward? You might say, "oh no, they will be rewarded; it is just not mentioned." Again, I will say it seems to me that the saints who missed rapture are more important before the eyes of God compared to the saints who made rapture. Because heaven took time out of its busy schedule to describe the reward that will be waiting for those who missed rapture but either forgot to mention the reward of those who made rapture or considered it not important enough to be mentioned.

Now then, those are questions we need to ask ourselves, but we have still not clarified much about the saints in question. So, let's look further in the passage for clues: Daniel 7:22,26:

> *22. Until the Ancient of days came, and judgment was given to the saints of the most High; and the time came that the saints possessed the kingdom. 26. But the judgment shall sit, and they shall take away his dominion, to consume and to destroy it unto the end.*

Notice what is said in these two verses. They are speaking of the same event. One says judgement has been given (Verse 22) and the other says that judgement shall sit (Verse 26). Who is giving the judgement? Who is going to sit at the judgement? Who are they going to judge? A lot of people think Jesus is going to be the only judge. No. Look at the passage again. Look at Verse 26 specifically. It says judgment shall sit and they shall . . . Who is they? That's a plural noun. It's definitely more than one judge. And it's not Jesus and the angels because the Bible says we shall judge angels (1 Corinthians 6:3). The "they" in that passage is Jesus and the saints. The saints are also going to be part of the judges. They are going to judge the entire evil done by the antichrist and other people in his administration (just like what was done immediately after World War II). They are also going to judge the rest of the world based on their attitude towards Israel during their most trying moment. Now then, we can clearly see that the saints are part of the judges but we are not clear on who the saints are. The next question we should ask is which saints? The ones that made the rapture before tribulation (if that is true) or the ones that missed the rapture and then managed through tribulation? Is there one group of saints or are there two groups (pre rapture and post rapture saints)?

Let's search elsewhere in the Bible for answers to the above questions. Look at 1 Corinthians 6:1–2:

> *1. Dare any of you, having a matter against another, go to law before the unjust, and not before the saints? 2. Do ye not know that the saints shall judge the world? and if the world shall be judged by you, are ye unworthy to judge the smallest matters?*

173

This is one of the letters of Paul to the Corinthian Church. He wrote this letter to them in order to address certain issues that were brought to him (in this same letter, he talks about rapture in Chapter 15). One of the issues was that the Christians in the Corinthian church took themselves to the court of law to settle their dispute. This was upsetting to him because he felt that they shouldn't have gone to civil court because unbelievers preside over it. He wrote this particular chapter to straighten them up. Notice what he says in Verse 2: Don't you know that the saints shall judge the world? Which saint is he referring to here? Notice that these are Christians who are expecting to be raptured. Paul categorically tells them that they will judge the world. How did Paul know that they will judge the world? He must have read the prophecy of Daniel. How sure are we that Paul read the prophecy of Daniel?

Paul was a pharisee (Pharisees are a sect of the leaders of the synagogue who are proficient in their knowledge of the Old Testament). He learnt the Torah (what we know as the Old Testament) under the best lawyer of his time (more like an Ivy league college) Gamaliel (Act 22:3). He wrote two-thirds of the entire New Testament Bible. In his writings, he quoted/paraphrased about two hundred Old Testament passages. That's aside from his references to people, places, and events in the Old Testament that he mentioned in his New Testament writings. He quoted/paraphrased the book of Daniel twice—apart from the one under consideration (1 Corinthians 15:3 - Is 53, Dan 9:26, Zec13:7 and 2 Thessalonians 2:4 – Dan 11:36)

Considering this resume of Paul, we can say beyond reasonable doubt that he had read the book of Daniel. If he did read the book of Daniel, then it is possible he got the information that the saints shall judge the world from the book of Daniel because that is about the only book where it is mentioned that the saints shall be part of the judgement that shall sit to judge the antichrist and his cohorts. So here, Paul has opened a whole new world of information. We now know that there is only one group of saints who will judge the world. The saints Paul refers to here are saints that were still waiting to be raptured. And yet they were being told they would judge the world.

Now then, the prophecy of Daniel doesn't say the (pre-tribulation) raptured saints will judge the world. It says the saints who will go through the great tribulation will judge the world. Paul and Daniel are definitely talking about the same group of saints. Therefore, there aren't two groups of saints, just one. Paul has shed some light on the saints. They are the saints waiting to be raptured, NOT the saints that have been raptured (there is nothing like that in the Scripture). Again, this goes to confirm that there will be no rapture before the great tribulation. There is only one group of saints—those that will go through the great tribulation and at the end, judge the world and angels. Again, we have seen Scriptures confirming Scriptures without any inferences. Therefore, the idea that the saints mentioned in Daniel are post-raptured saints is unbiblical. It is NOT written anywhere in the Bible that there will be saints left after the rapture. It is another doctrine coined out of human imagination to support a narrative. No Bible passage supports the idea.

John also mentions the saints being afflicted by the antichrist (the great tribulation). Look at Revelation 13:7:

> *7. And it was given unto him to make war with the saints, and to overcome them: and power was given him over all kindreds, and tongues, and nations.*

Notice how John puts it in this passage. The antichrist shall make war with the saints. Only one group of saints. It doesn't say the left-behind saints or the post-raptured saints. He says "the saints" because there is only one group of saints—those that will go through the great tribulation, be raptured, and at the end, judge the world with Christ. Now we have three viable witnesses with four accounts. Jesus, Paul, and Daniel (in two passages) attest that the antichrist will be revealed, and there will be the great tribulation before rapture. Daniel goes a little further by giving us how long the tribulation will last.

Daniel again sheds some more light on the matter in Daniel Chapter 11, making it the third account from Daniel we shall be considering. Let us look at it to see if it is similar to Daniel 7. In Daniel 11, greater details are made known. Although this is a pretty long passage, we shall look at the verses that have to do with our topic of discussion. Daniel 11:29–45, 12:1–3:

29. At the time appointed he shall return, and come toward the south; but it shall not be as the former, or as the latter. 30. For the ships of Chittim shall come against him: therefore he shall be grieved, and return, and have indignation against the holy covenant: so shall he do; he shall even return, and have intelligence with them that forsake the holy covenant. 31. And arms shall stand on his part, and they shall pollute the sanctuary of strength, and shall take away the daily sacrifice, and they shall place the abomination that maketh desolate.

Too much to digest here, but let's summarize as much as possible for better understanding. First, in this passage, the antichrist is referred to as the king of the north. This is because Jerusalem is positioned in such a way that the country of origin or the kingdom of the antichrist is on the north of Jerusalem. Look at the following examples: Ezekiel 38:6–8, 16:

6. Gomer, and all his bands; the house of Togarmah of the north quarters, and all his bands: and many people with thee. 7. Be thou prepared, and prepare for thyself, thou, and all thy company that are assembled unto thee, and be thou a guard unto them. 8. After many days thou shalt be visited: in the latter years thou shalt come into the land that is brought back from the sword,

> *and is gathered out of many people, against the*
> *mountains of Israel, which have been always waste:*
> *but it is brought forth out of the nations, and they shall*
> *dwell safely all of them. 16. And thou shalt come up*
> *against my people of Israel, as a cloud to cover the*
> *land; it shall be in the latter days, and I will bring thee*
> *against my land, that the heathen may know me, when*
> *I shall be sanctified in thee, O Gog, before their eyes.*

In the above passages, Gog, which is the name given to the
antichrist in this particular prophecy, will be invading Israel from the
north quarters. Look at another passage: Ezekiel 39:1–2:

> *1. Therefore, thou son of man, prophesy against*
> *Gog, and say, Thus saith the Lord GOD; Behold, I*
> *am against thee, O Gog, the chief prince of*
> *Meshech and Tubal: 2. And I will turn thee back,*
> *and leave but the sixth part of thee, and will cause*
> *thee to come up from the north parts, and will*
> *bring thee upon the mountains of Israel:*

Notice also, that in this passage, the antichrist and his army
will invade Israel from the north parts. Hence, the king of the north
referred to in Daniel 11 is the same as the antichrist. Now then, let's go
back to Daniel 11. Now notice what is said about the antichrist in
Verses 30 and 31:

178

30. For the ships of Chittim shall come against him: therefore he shall be grieved, and return, and have indignation against the holy covenant: so shall he do; he shall even return, and have intelligence with them that forsake the holy covenant. 31. And arms shall stand on his part, and they shall pollute the sanctuary of strength, and shall take away the daily sacrifice, and they shall place the abomination that maketh desolate.

First, he was mad against the Holy covenant and then he went to set up the abomination that maketh desolate. This also confirms to us that the king of the north is the antichrist. This is exactly how Jesus introduces him in Matthew 24. Look at it in Verse 15:

15. When ye therefore shall see the abomination of desolation, spoken of by Daniel the prophet, stand in the holy place, (whoso readeth, let him understand:)

This abomination will be set up in the temple by the antichrist. So, let's go on with Daniel 11:32–34:

32. And such as do wickedly against the covenant shall he corrupt by flatteries: but the people that do know their God shall be strong, and do exploits. 33. And they that understand among the people shall instruct many: yet they shall fall by the sword, and by flame, by captivity, and by spoil, many days.

179

Notice Verses 32 and 33. Despite the attempt of the antichrist to deceive the world with his flatteries, some among the people who know their God will be able to see through his flatteries and resist him. And they will do exploit. Now look at Verse 33. And they that understand among the people shall instruct many. What could that possibly mean? What do they understand? Now, this is the whole essence of having these prophecies written down: It is so that the generation of Christians who will be alive during that time will read and understand the time and season in which they are. Understanding brings preparation, and preparation makes it possible to stand at the time of difficulty. I give you an example. Look at the ants, they prepare their food and their homes during summer. This is because they know that winter is coming and during winter, due to the harshness of the weather, it is impossible to go around and look for food. Hence, if they must survive the winter, they must prepare during summer. That is the ant. If they are wise enough to prepare for themselves and their family when the weather is good in order to survive when the weather is harsh, then humans should be able to do better. That is why the passage says those that understand among the people. It means they have read the Bible and digested all about the matter of the end time. They understand what is coming upon humanity during this time. A time they won't be able to buy or sell because of their faith in Christ. Then they need to prepare for themselves and their family during this period. These are the people that will now begin to instruct other Christians about the times and season in which they are.

Notice also, in the same verse, the Bible tells what manner of persecution (great tribulation) will be brought on those who understand: they shall fall by the sword. Whose sword? The antichrist's sword. What else does the prophecy say about them? Some shall be burnt, some will be imprisoned, some will be raped, some bitten, etc. And this will happen for many days. It is clear in these two verses that not all Christians who will be alive then will have a proper understanding of the times and season they are in. Although it is the will of God that all come to the understanding of the times they are in (this is the major reason why it is written down by many prophets in many ways), the devil wants to leave us unprepared, and hence he will attempt to darken the understanding of many. This is why it is very critical to know exactly what the Bible says about the timing of rapture.

Now let's go further: Daniel 11:34–35:

> *34. Now when they shall fall, they shall be holpen with a little help: but many shall cleave to them with flatteries. 35. And some of them of understanding shall fall, to try them, and to purge, and to make them white, even to the time of the end: because it is yet for a time appointed.*

Notice that Verses 34 and 35 are a continuation of what is ntroduced in Verses 32 and 33. Notice that Verse 34 says they are going to be helped with a little help. The manner of help being described here is more or less like helping them to cope with the level of persecution because it will be so difficult that no flesh will be able to survive it. Look at what Jesus says about it in Matthew 24:21–22:

> *21. For then shall be great tribulation, such as was not since the beginning of the world to this time, no, nor ever shall be. 22. And except those days should be shortened, there should no flesh be saved: but for the elect's sake those days shall be shortened.*

Now, God, in His infinite mercy, shows us why there will be that level of persecution. Notice what is said in Verse 35 of Daniel 11. The reason for the persecution is to purge the Christians and to make them white. This is the exact thing said concerning the Christians who will go through this period in the book of Revelation: Revelation 7:13–14:

> *13. And one of the elders answered, saying unto me, What are these which are arrayed in white robes? and whence came they? 14. And I said unto him, Sir, thou knowest. And he said to me, These are they which came out of great tribulation, and have washed their robes and made them white in the blood of the Lamb.*

Did you notice the response of the elder to the question? The are the ones who came out of the great tribulation and they have washed their robes through the tribulation and it is now white. In the mouth of two or three witnesses, every word shall be established. The same exact thing Daniel is trying to communicate in Daniel 11:34. Now let's move on. From Verse 35 down to Verse 45, Daniel speaks extensively about the acts of the antichrist. This is beyond the scope of this book, hence we shall not talk about it. Moving forward, we shall consider Daniel 12:1–2:

> *1. And at that time shall Michael stand up, the great prince which standeth for the children of thy people: and there shall be a time of trouble, such as never was since there was a nation even to that same time: and at that time thy people shall be delivered, every one that shall be found written in the book. 2. And many of them that sleep in the dust of the earth shall awake, some to everlasting life, and some to shame and everlasting contempt.*

The first thing to note before looking at these verses is that the original Bible is not written in verses and chapters. It is written as a book. The translators have added verses and chapters for easy reference. Hence, Chapter 12 is just a continuation of what is being said in Chapter 11 without the numbers. Now then, Verse 1 tells us how great the trouble will be for both Israel and for us Christians. The reason why Michael, the angel over the nation, will arise is because

183

the antichrist will direct his army to the nation Israel. His attempt will be to accomplish the plan that the devil has been trying to achieve since Israel became a nation—wipe the Israelis off the face of the earth (Daniel 11:41). This is completely different from the persecution that all Christians worldwide will go through during this same time period (that was what we considered in Daniel 11:30–34). Now, consider what happens in Verse 2 of Chapter 12. While the attack on the nation Israel, through the army of the antichrist physically present in Israel, is going on, and while the worldwide persecution is going on against Christians, suddenly this will happen. Note what Daniel says in Verse 2: He says many that sleep in the dust shall awake. Doesn't that sound familiar? Let's check it out in one of our New Testament passages: 1 Thessalonians 4:16:

> *16. For the Lord himself shall descend from heaven with a shout, with the voice of the archangel, and with the trump of God: and the dead in Christ shall rise first:*

Notice how Paul puts it. The dead in Christ will rise from their grave while Daniel says many that sleep in the dust shall awake. Can you see that? The next question is, what phenomenon does this describe? This is the rapture.

Now then, if we are to summarize Daniel 11:29–45, and 12:1–2, we can put it like this: When the antichrist comes, he will desecrate the temple of God in Jerusalem by putting an abomination that makes desolate (what that is, we cannot tell for now). Then he will persecute the Christians with the kind of persecution the world has never seen before because they will be seen as the enemy of the state, anti-whatever they choose to call it at that time, mis-informant etc. (Remember also that at this time the mark will be enforced. And only those with the proper understanding of the times and season will refuse the mark. They will lose their jobs and livelihood and will easily be seen as people against societal development or whatever). While the antichrist is doing this, he will seek to accomplish his long-time dream of wiping out the nation of Israel from the world map. Then the Lord will show up and first rapture His beloved before unleashing His destruction on the army. This narrative is exactly similar to the narrative of Paul we looked at and the narrative of Jesus and of John the author of the book of Revelation.

Now, going back to Daniel 7:19–27, we can easily see that it will be a Herculean task to try to prove that the saints mentioned here (Daniel 7:19–27) are those who missed the rapture. It is clear here, putting Daniel 7 and Daniel 11 together, that there is only one rapture and that that rapture comes after the tribulation of those days (Daniel 12). This is also in line with what Jesus and Paul say in Matthew and Thessalonians, respectively. So, we have three witnesses with five references pointing out the same truths—until the antichrist comes on the scene and unleashes the great tribulation upon Christians, rapture will not occur.

Now then, someone might say, "You've got it all mixed up. Daniel 11 is referring to Antiochus Epiphanes who desecrated the temple." Well, that is a credible observation and in order to accept the third account of Daniel as a viable witness, we must look into the matter and clarify it.

To understand Daniel 7 and Daniel 11, one needs to first look at Daniel 2, Nebuchadnezzar's dream. In this dream, all the major empires the world would ever know, starting from Nebuchadnezzar down to the antichrist, are mentioned in succession. Daniel 2:32-33:

> *32. This image's head was of fine gold, his breast and his arms of silver, his belly and his thighs of brass, 33. His legs of iron, his feet part of iron and part of clay.*

Notice the way the dream is structured. Five major kingdoms on earth before the second coming of Christ. Each kingdom is represented by a part of the image (which is in human form) Nebuchadnezzar sees in his dream. The head is made of gold and represents the Babylonian kingdom. The dream does not tell how many kings will rule in Babylon before the breast and the arms kingdom takes over. It is the same with the others. The dream does not tell how many kings will rule the Medo-Persian kingdom before the Greeks take over. The vision in Daniel 11 does not mention the name of the kingdoms like Daniel 2 does. However, Daniel 11 talks about kings in each kingdom and the major events carried out by these kings. Starting from the kings of Median and Persian (who are the part of the image that is in power at that time), the angel tells Daniel about all the major kings and the major events within their reign, up until the second coming of Christ, without mentioning the kingdoms as mentioned in Daniel 2.

Now then, Antiochus Epiphanes was a Greek Hellenistic king who ascended the throne at eighteen and restored most of the territories of the Seleucid empire before his death in 164 BC. He desecrated the temple by offering the sacrifice of a pig to Zeus on an altar after the Greeks came the Roman empire to take over the same areas ruled by Antiochus. Also of note is that both the Babylonian kings and the Medo-Persian kings ruled over the same territories. After Alexander the Great, the territories were divided into four major regions based on his four generals who succeeded him. They continued until the Romans took over these same regions. Hence, when the angel is describing the series of events that will come to pass concerning the end time prophecies, he doesn't change the region. He just uses south and north based on the empire's position to Jerusalem.

Now then, let us look very critically at the prophecy in Daniel 11 and compare it to the life of Antiochus IV Epiphanes. I will just highlight the major differences between Antiochus Epiphanes and the antichrist. According to Daniel 11, the antichrist will gain entrance into Jerusalem with a great army and with a great force: Daniel 11:40–41:

40. And at the time of the end shall the king of the south push at him: and the king of the north shall come against him like a whirlwind, with chariots, and with horsemen, and with many ships; and he shall enter into the countries, and shall overflow and pass over. 41. He shall enter also into the glorious land, and many countries shall be overthrown: but these shall escape out of his hand, even Edom, and Moab, and the chief of the children of Ammon.

But according to the Jewish author Josephus in his book, the antiquities of the Jews, Antiochus gained entrance into Jerusalem by treachery. According to Daniel 11, the antichrist will not worship or force people to worship any god. He will project himself as god and demand worship. See that in Daniel 11:36–37:

36. And the king shall do according to his will; and he shall exalt himself, and magnify himself above every god, and shall speak marvellous things against the God of gods, and shall prosper till the indignation be accomplished: for that that is determined shall be done. 37. Neither shall he regard the God of his fathers, nor the desire of women, nor regard any god for he shall magnify himself above all.

But according to history, Antiochus Epiphanes worshipped

several gods, one of whom was Zeus, and he forced the people to build temples and raise idol altars in every city and village and offer swine upon them every day. Lastly, the abomination of desolation mentioned in Daniel 11:31 was repeated by Jesus about two hundred years after Antiochus Epiphanes died. That tells us that there is another abomination of desolation yet to come, that will be set up in the future temple by the antichrist.

Now then, the next logical question to consider is, does the Bible talk about Antiochus Epiphanes at all? Definitely. Antiochus Epiphanes is the prototype of the antichrist. Hence, there are many similarities between him and the antichrist. Antiochus Epiphanes came just before the first coming of Jesus, while the antichrist will come just before the second coming of Jesus (we can as well say Antiochus was the first coming of the antichrist, and the antichrist will be the second coming). Look at how Daniel introduces Antiochus in Daniel 8:8–9:

> *8. Therefore the he goat waxed very great: and when he was strong, the great horn was broken; and for it came up four notable ones toward the four winds of heaven. 9. And out of one of them **came forth a little horn**, which waxed exceeding great, toward the south, and toward the east, and toward the pleasant land.*

In the passage above, there is a he goat that has a strong horn. He waxes very great. That is Alexander the Great. Notice what happens when the horn is broken. Four notable horns come out of the great horn that is broken. These represent the four generals that divided the kingdom of Alexander amongst themselves. From one of these generals comes a little horn that represents Antiochus Epiphany. But the antichrist is represented differently in Daniel 7:7–8:

> *7. After this I saw in the night visions, and behold a fourth beast, dreadful and terrible, and strong exceedingly; and it had great iron teeth: it devoured and brake in pieces, and stamped the residue with the feet of it: and it was diverse from all the beasts that were before it; and it had ten horns. 8. I considered the horns, and, behold, there came up among them another little horn, before whom there were three of the first horns plucked up by the roots: and, behold, in this horn were eyes like the eyes of man, and a mouth speaking great things.*

Notice that this particular little horn talked about in Chapter 7 comes out of the remnants of the Roman empire, which was divided into ten horns, while the little horn in Chapter 8 comes out of one of the four horns (Alexander's four generals who took over the empire after his demise) of the he goat (Alexander the Great). They can't be speaking about the same person. The one in Chapter 8 talks about

Antiochus while the one in Chapter 7 talks about the antichrist. Hence, Antiochus is a prototype of the antichrist, with similar characteristics. This is God's way of giving us a precedence so we can have an idea of how the reign of the antichrist will be.

Antiochus desecrated the temple by offering pigs to Zeus, and Daniel refers to the act as "the transgression of desolation" in Verse 13 of Daniel 8, where Antiochus is talked about;

> *13. Then I heard one saint speaking, and another saint said unto that certain saint which spake, How long shall be the vision concerning the daily sacrifice, and the **transgression of desolation**, to give both the sanctuary and the host to be trodden under foot?*

The antichrist will also desecrate the temple by setting up an image in the temple and Daniel calls this the abomination that maketh desolate in Daniel 11:31:

> *31. And arms shall stand on his part, and they shall pollute the sanctuary of strength, and shall take away the daily sacrifice, and they shall place the **abomination that maketh desolate**.*

Antiochus stopped the daily sacrifice in the temple, as recorded in Daniel 8:11;

> *11. Yea, he magnified himself even to the prince of the host, and by him the **daily sacrifice was taken away,** and the place of his sanctuary was cast down.*

The antichrist will also stop the daily sacrifice that will be going on in the future temple: Daniel 11:31:

> *31. And arms shall stand on his part, and they shall pollute the sanctuary of strength, **and shall take away the daily sacrifice,** and they shall place the abomination that maketh desolate.*

Antiochus persecuted Israel for 2,300 days, as recorded in Daniel 8:13–14:

> *13. Then I heard one saint speaking, and another saint said unto that certain saint which spake, How long shall be the vision concerning the daily sacrifice, and the transgression of desolation, to give both the sanctuary and the host to be trodden under foot? 14 And he said unto me, **Unto two thousand and three hundred days;** then shall the sanctuary be cleansed.*

The antichrist will persecute Israel for three and a half years as recorded in Daniel 7:25:

> *25 And he shall speak great words against the most*

*High, and shall wear out the saints of the most High,
and think to change times and laws: and they shall be
given into his hand until a time and times and the
dividing of time.*

From the above analysis, we can see beyond all reasonable
doubt that Antiochus is definitely not the one being referred to in
Daniel Chapters 7 and 11. We can also see the clear differences
between the two characters (Antiochus and antichrist) from the
Scriptures shown.

Now then, so far, we have seen, beyond all reasonable doubt,
that the book of Daniel is very clear on the timing of rapture. It is
clearly stated without any ambiguity that the Christians will be here
while the antichrist is being revealed, as will they be here during the
great tribulation, and rapture will only happen at the tail end of the
great tribulation, which will last for three and a half years.

The next thing to do now is to compare our findings in the
book of Daniel about rapture to what we have learnt from the writings
of Paul and from the Gospels to see if they are all saying the same
thing. Let's compare the timeline Paul gives to the one Jesus and
Daniel give: 2 Thessalonians 2:3:

*3. Let no man deceive you by any means: for that
day shall not come, **except** there come a **falling***

> *away first, and that **man of sin be revealed**, the son*
> *of perdition.*

The above passage is simple and clear. Two things must happen before the rapture takes place. One, many Christians will abandon their religion/faith/backslide and second, the antichrist will come on scene. This is exactly the same timeline Jesus and Daniel give. Look at it: Matthew 24:12,15,29–30:

> *12. And many false prophets shall rise, and shall*
> *deceive many. And because iniquity shall abound, **the***
> ***love of many shall wax cold**. 15. When ye therefore*
> *shall **see the abomination of desolation**, spoken of by*
> *Daniel the prophet, stand in the holy place, (whoso*
> *readeth, let him understand:). 29. **Immediately after***
> ***the tribulation** of those days shall the sun be*
> *darkened, and the moon shall not give her light, and*
> *the stars shall fall from heaven, and the powers of the*
> *heavens shall be shaken: 30. And then shall appear the*
> *sign of the Son of man in heaven: and then shall all the*
> *tribes of the earth mourn, and they shall see the Son of*
> *man coming in the clouds of heaven with power and*
> *great glory. 31. And he shall send his angels with a*
> ***great sound of a trumpet**, and they **shall gathe***
> ***together his elect** from the four winds, from one end of*
> *heaven to the other.*

Look at how Daniel puts it: Daniel 11:32, 33, 36, 12:2:

> *32. And such as do wickedly against the covenant shall he corrupt by flatteries: but the people that do know their God shall be strong, and do exploits (KJV). 32. By deceit the king will win the support of those who have **already abandoned their religion,** but those who follow God will fight back (GNB). 33. And they that understand among the people shall instruct many: yet they shall **fall by the sword, and by flame, by captivity, and by spoil, many days**. 36. And **the king** shall do according to his will; and he shall exalt himself, and magnify himself above every god, and shall speak marvellous things against the God of gods, and shall prosper till the indignation be accomplished: for that that is determined shall be done. 12:2. And **many of them that sleep in the dust of the earth shall awake,** some to everlasting life, and some to shame and everlasting contempt.*

Compare all three without any form of human input. They are saying exactly the same things. There must be a great fall away first, then the antichrist will be revealed to unleash the great tribulation upon Christians and to attempt to annihilate Israel before rapture can occur. I don't think it can be any clearer. So far, we can see that no inferences needed to be made before any conclusion was reached. No one can argue against the truth.

195

Chapter 15

Revelation 7 Truth

The book of Revelation is a very unique book. It is difficult to understand. But glory be to God, the Lamb has prevailed and has unsealed the book: Revelation 5:5:

> *5. And one of the elders saith unto me, Weep not: behold, the Lion of the tribe of Juda, the Root of David, hath prevailed to open the book, **and to loose the seven seals thereof.***

Some people still believe it is impossible to understand it because it is a sealed book. I beg to differ. If it is not unsealed, Chapters 6 through 22 should not exist. The book should immediately stop at Chapter 5. But because Jesus has unsealed it, we can read about the seals from Chapters 6 through 22. I believe we can understand enough to help us prepare for what is coming. Having said that, it should also be noted that there are some parts of the book of Revelation that are still sealed and deliberately so. Heaven decided not to unseal them. And in such cases, heaven clearly informs us that this part is sealed until certain times. Let's consider such an example Revelation 10:4:

> *3. And when the seven thunders had uttered their voices, I was about to write: and I heard a voice from heaven saying unto me, **Seal up those thing** which the seven thunders uttered, and write them not.*

Did you notice what heaven says in that passage concerning the voices of the seven thunders? Heaven commands John not to write. Those voices must remain sealed. It's supposed to be kept from human understanding. This also goes to support my earlier point. The book of Revelation is not entirely sealed. Jesus has unsealed it for the most part so we can understand His purpose for the end time and live our lives accordingly. We are clearly informed about the portions that are still sealed. So, it is wrong for anyone to go about teaching that the book of Revelation is not meant to be understood.

Another thing about the book of Revelation is that the chapters are not written in chronological order. What this means is that you cannot say, for example, events in Chapter 1 happened before the events in Chapter 2. Sometimes you can find that the events in Chapter 13 happened before those in Chapter 7 (that's just an example). However, certain parts are in chronological order. For example, the seals. When the book mentions the first seal, then what must come next is the second seal. Hence, all the chapters that talk about the unfolding of the seals are sequential. For example, John starts talking about the seals in Chapter 5 and continues through to Chapter 7. This means that the events mentioned in Chapters 5, 6, and 7 are in chronological order. The same thing goes for the trumpets that were sounded. The first trumpet will naturally sound before the second. Hence, all the chapters where the blowing of the trumpets is talked about are in chronological order except in a few instances when there is a break in between to talk about something else before returning to the sounds.

Now then, we are starting our search from Chapter 7 because it is the first instance in the book of Revelation where saints are mentioned to appear in heaven. Chapters 1 through 3 are about correction and information for the church in the days of John. Though we can learn some lessons from them, they are written for our learning, but they are not part of the end time prophecies. The prophecy starts from Chapter 4 onwards, with John appearing in heaven. A lot of people have equated that to be the rapture of the church. That is not rapture. John is not the church, neither can he be taken to represent the church because the passage doesn't state that. He was not even the head of the church during his days. He was only taken to heaven in the spirit, and the text specifically mentions that. Look at it: Revelation chapter 4:1–2:

> 1.After this I looked, and, behold, a door was opened in heaven: and the first voice which I heard was as it were of a trumpet talking with me; which said, Come up hither, and I will shew thee things which must be hereafter. 2. And immediately **I was in the spirit**: and behold, a throne was set in heaven, and one sat on the throne.

Did you see that in Verse 2? The text also specifically mentions that he alone is taken to heaven in the spirit. No one else is with him. Rapture will not occur in the spirit. There is no passage talking about rapture that says it will occur in the spirit. It is a physical thing. The whole world will notice we have gone. They will know people are missing. It will not occur in the spirit. In fact, we shall go with our new body. In that event, John's physical body was on the island of Patmos. People around him could still see him.

Now then, going back to the events recorded in Chapter 7 of the book of Revelation. These events occurred just before the seventh seal was opened. That means that these series of events in Chapter 7 occurred after the events of the first through the sixth seal had played out on earth. So, let's look at it to see if we can get some clues. Revelation 7:1–3

> *1. And after these things I saw four angels standing on the four corners of the earth, holding the four winds of the earth, that the wind should not blow on the earth, nor on the sea, nor on any tree. 2. And I saw another angel ascending from the east, having the seal of the living God: and he cried with a loud voice to the four angels, to whom it was given to hurt the earth and the sea, 3. Saying, Hurt not the earth, neither the sea, nor the trees, till we have sealed the servants of our God in their foreheads.*

Notice how that chapter starts with ". . . after these things." Which things, one might wonder. The things that happened after the first seal through the sixth seal were opened. One would expect the seventh seal to follow immediately, but there is a pause. What could be the reason for the pause? Look at Verse 3. There we have the reason for the pause. The servants of God have to be sealed on their foreheads before God unleashes His wrath on the earth. That will lead us to other questions. Does it mean the other seals are not the wrath of God? What then could those seals be?

Let's do a mini review of the first six seals to see what they actually are. Starting with first seal: Revelation 6:1–2:

> *1. And I saw when the Lamb opened one of the seals, and I heard, as it were the noise of thunder, one of the four beasts saying, Come and see. 2. And I saw, and behold a white horse: and he that sat on him had a bow; and a crown **was given unto him** and he went forth conquering, and to conquer.*

Notice what happens when the first seal is opened. A white horse comes running with a rider on it. This white horse is not Jesus, neither does it signify a good omen because it is white (we can't tell much about that because that is not our current focus). Take note of the phrase used for the rider: "a crown was given unto him." By whom? To do what? The Bible doesn't state who has given him the crown but states the reason for the crown. That term "given unto him" is used majorly in relation to the antichrist's activities. Look at this example: Revelation 13:5a:

> 5.*And there **was given unto him** a mouth speaking great things and blasphemies;*

Notice the same phrase in this passage: "given unto him." It doesn't state who has given, but what has been given is an ability to carry out a specific assignment. Hence, the first seal is not God's wrath. It is someone empowered to carry out certain specific havoc on earth. Whatever it is that has empowered that personality is not named. But it is clear that this havoc is not from God. The point I am trying to make may not be very clear now. But as we go further, it will get clearer. Let's look at the second seal: Revelation 6:3–4:

> 3. *And when he had opened the second seal, I heard the second beast say, Come and see. 4. And there went out another horse that was red: **and power was given to him** that sat thereon to take peace from the earth, and that they should kill one another: and there was given unto him a great sword.*

Notice what happens when the second seal is opened. A red horse with a rider comes forth. Notice the same phrase again: "power was given to him." By whom? We do not know. But if you look at

201

Revelation 13, where some of the activities of the antichrist are mentioned, you will again see the same phrase. Revelation 13:5b:

> *5. And there was given unto him a mouth speaking great things and blasphemies; **and power was given unto** him to continue forty and two months.*

Notice the same phrase: "and power was given unto him." Also notice the evil the rider is empowered to unleash on the earth. Again, you can see that that is not God's wrath (when we start looking at the seventh seal, we shall understand better). Again, let's look at the third seal. Revelation 6:5–6:

> *5. And when he had opened the third seal, I heard the third beast say, Come and see. And I beheld, and lo a black horse; and he that sat on him had a pair of balances in his hand. 6. And I heard a voice in the midst of the four beasts say, A measure of wheat for a penny, and three measures of barley for a penny; and see thou hurt not the oil and the wine.*

Notice what happens when this particular seal is opened. Although it is not stated that power is given to him, but we can clearly see that power is given to him. And it is definitely the same personality that has given the first two horses power that also gives this black horse rider power. What is of note here is that this particular horse is only given a limitation by a voice from the midst of the four beasts. Again, we have seen this kind of pattern before. In the case of the devil and Job. The devil is only given an area of limitation beyond which he cannot go. Look at it in Job 1:12:

> *12. And the LORD said unto Satan, Behold, all that he hath is in thy power;* **only upon himself put not forth thine hand.** *So Satan went forth from the presence of the LORD.*

Notice what God says to the devil. The devil is only given a limitation. He has the power but a boundary is created within that he cannot go beyond when he perpetuates his act. The same is with the rider that comes forth from the opening of the third seal. Hence, this rider has unlimited ability to create famine on earth. But God, in His graciousness, gives him a boundary beyond which he cannot go. Again, we can see in this situation that the evil act is not from God but permitted by God. The rider is deriving his power from another personality. This is not the wrath of God.

Now let's consider the fourth seal. Revelation 6:7–8:

> *7. And when he had opened the fourth seal, I heard the voice of the fourth beast say, Come and see. 8. And I looked, and behold a pale horse: and his name that sat on him was Death, and Hell followed with him.* **And**

power was given unto them over the fourth part of the earth, to kill with sword, and with hunger, and with death, and with the beasts of the earth.

Now then, the fourth seal ushers in two riders—death and hell. Notice also the same phrase: "power was given unto them," It means all the riders got their powers from the same source. That source seems to be obsessed with unleashing evil on earth. Now let's look at the fifth seal. Revelation 6:9:

9. And when he had opened the fifth seal, I saw under the altar the souls of them that were slain for the word of God, and for the testimony which they held:

This seal is also reported a little differently from the rest of the seals (just like the third seal). Here, we see that the person who was unveiled when this seal was opened was given power to kill the saints. Which was what was evidence under the altar when the seal was opened.

Now, the sixth seal was opened and we see a new dimension here Revelation 6:12:

12. And I beheld when he had opened the sixth seal and, lo, there was a great earthquake; and the sun became black as sackcloth of hair, and the moon became as blood.

Here, the earth is showing the then inhabitant of the earth a sign of the things to come. What is a sign? When you are traveling in your car, there are road signs that tell you that you are on the right track to your destination. The signs are not your destination, but they are pointers to show you where your destination is. The same is with the sixth seal. It is not the main event; it is a sign to show that the main event is coming. The next logical question is what is the destination this particular sign is pointing to? Let us consider the rest of the passages: Revelation 6:12–17:

> *12. And I beheld when he had opened the sixth seal, and, lo, there was a great earthquake; and the sun became black as sackcloth of hair, and the moon became as blood; 13. And the stars of heaven fell unto the earth, even as a fig tree casteth her untimely figs, when she is shaken of a mighty wind. 14. And the heaven departed as a scroll when it is rolled together; and every mountain and island were moved out of their places. 15. And the kings of the earth, and the great men, and the rich men, and the chief captains, and the mighty men, and every bondman, and every free man, hid themselves in the dens and in the rocks of the mountains; 16. And said to the mountains and rocks, Fall on us, and hide us from the face of him that sitteth on the throne, and from the wrath of the Lamb: 17. For the great day of his wrath is come; and who shall be able to stand?*

Look at what is happening in these passages. The earth is quaking, the sun is refusing to give its light, the moon is changing its color, the stars of heaven are falling unto the earth, the heavens (firmament) are departing as if someone is rolling off a rug from the floor, and mountains are beginning to move from their original position. Why all these movements? It just seems these things, like living things, know that something terrible is about to happen. Notice that all the things that happened in the last five seals were targeted directly towards humans. But here, the earth and other creations seem to know that the next set of events that are coming are coming from the one who created them and it's going to be grievous for all—both living and non-living things. The reaction we see above from these elements are a sign of things to come. Again, see Verse 15. Even humans seem to know what is coming. Notice that the humans are not hiding from what has already happened in Verses 12 through 14. They are hiding from what they believe is going to happen or what is yet to come but certain to come. Look at Verse 17. The great day of the Lord, which is the day of His wrath, is what is coming next. How then do we know that what has happened in Verses 12 through 15 is a sign of things to come? Let's look at other passages where these same events are recorded; Joel 2:30–31:

> 30. And I will shew wonders in the heavens and in the earth, blood, and fire, and pillars of smoke. 31. The sun shall be turned into darkness, and the moon into blood, before the great and the terrible day of the LORD come.

206

Notice how the same event is described in the above verses. Notice the first statement in Verse 30. God says He will show wonders in heaven and on earth. When? Look at Verse 31. Just before the great and terrible day of the Lord. What is the great and terrible day of the Lord? That is the day the Lord will start pouring His wrath on earth. The events in Verse 30 and first part of Verse 31 are signs of things to come (the wrath of God). It is the same as we saw when the sixth seal was opened. The events that occurred are signs of what is to come. This clearly means that the first through the fifth seals are not the wrath of God. They are directed towards humans by some powers. And notice the fifth seal is specifically directed towards the saints.

Let's look at another example in Luke 21:25:

> *25. And there shall be signs in the sun, and in the moon, and in the stars; and upon the earth distress of nations, with perplexity; the sea and the waves roaring; 26. Men's hearts failing them for fear, and for looking after those things which are coming on the earth: for the powers of heaven shall be shaken.*

Notice how the above passage puts it. There shall be signs . . . This was the exact event John saw when the sixth seal was unsealed. Can you see that Jesus is calling it signs of things to come? Hence, the sixth seal is a sign of things to come—the unleashing of the wrath of God on earth.

Going back to Revelation 7:1–3 where we started from, we can now gain more understanding of what those verses are saying. Look at them again;

> *1, And after these things I saw four angels standing on the four corners of the earth, holding the four winds of the earth, that the wind should not blow on the earth, nor on the sea, nor on any tree. 2. And I saw another angel ascending from the east, having the seal of the living God: and he cried with a loud voice to the four angels, to whom it was given to hurt the earth and the sea, 3. Saying, Hurt not the earth, neither the sea, nor the trees, till we have sealed the servants of our God in their foreheads.*

After these things. Which things? The events that followed after the first through the fifth seals were unsealed (part of which includes the great tribulation) and the sign of the things to come which is the sixth seal. Notice Verse 3. The next thing that should come on earth is the unleashing of the wrath of God upon man. Notice that an angel is trying to stop another angel from unleashing God's wrath on earth until the servants of God are sealed. Why is this? Christians are subject to tribulation from the antichrist, but Christian are not subject to the wrath of God. Look at it in this passage; Thessalonians 5:9:

9. For God hath not appointed us to wrath, but to obtain salvation by our Lord Jesus Christ,

God has not appointed us to His wrath. You see that? That is why the second angel had to stop the first in his track. Now then, is rapture a seal? No. When God sends an angel to seal from His wrath, it just means the angel puts a mark on the followers of God so that when the angel that will unleash the wrath of God comes on earth, he will spare the sealed ones. Look at an example in Ezekiel 9:4–6:

> *4. And the LORD said unto him, Go through the midst of the city, through the midst of Jerusalem, and set **a mark upon the foreheads of the men** that sigh and that cry for all the abominations that be done in the midst thereof. 5. And to the others he said in mine hearing, Go ye after him through the city, and smite: let not your eye spare, neither have ye pity: 6. Slay utterly old and young, both maids, and little children, and women: but **come not near any man upon whom is the mark**; and begin at my sanctuary. Then they began at the ancient men which were before the house.*

Notice where the mark is placed. On the foreheads of the men who sighed for the sin of Jerusalem. Notice also that the angel that is to unleash the wrath of God on the people is instructed not to touch those who have the seal of God on their forehead. Hence, the point of sealing is not to take them out of the world via rapture or any other means. The point is to protect them from the wrath of God. Now then, going back to Revelation 7:3:

> *3. Saying, Hurt not the earth, neither the sea, nor the trees, till we have sealed the servants of our God in their foreheads.*

Notice where the seal is placed. On the forehead of the servants of God. Who are these servants of God? Those who sigh for the sins of the land. Now the number of them that are sealed is mentioned. But if you notice, that is only Jewish people. Look at it in Revelation 7:4:

> *4. And I heard the number of them which were sealed: and there were sealed an hundred and forty and four thousand **of all the tribes of the children of Israel.***

So, we can see that the first set of people sealed are all Israelites. Now then, look at Verse 9; Revelation 7:9:

> *9. After this I beheld, and, lo, a great multitude, which no man could number, of all nations, and kindreds, and people, and tongues, stood before the throne, and before the Lamb, clothed with white robes, and palm in their hands;*

After what? After sealing the Israelites that fear God. Notice what happens after the Israelites are sealed. A multitude of people from all nations of the earth are also shielded from the wrath of God because they fear God. But here the passage says they are those who stand before the throne with palms in their hands. Look at the further description given about this multitude; Revelation 7:13–14:

> *13. And one of the elders answered, saying unto me, What are these which are arrayed in white robes? and whence came they? 14. And I said unto him, Sir, thou knowest. And he said to me, These are **they which came out of great tribulation**, and have washed their robes, and made them white in the blood of the Lamb.*

Notice how the elder responds to his own question. He asks John who are these multitude of men seen in white who are sealed from the wrath of God just after the 144,000 Israelites are sealed? They are those who came out of the great tribulation. Did you see that? They suffered the tribulation of the antichrist but were either taken out or marked out of God's destruction. This is in line with all passages we have observed. Christians will go through the great tribulation but not the wrath of God. Again, just in case someone says these are the saints who will miss rapture, we have proven beyond reasonable doubt that there is only one group of saints, those that will go through the great tribulation. And those are the saints that will be raptured. We saw that in Daniel Chapters 7 and 11, and we saw that in 1 Corinthians.

Now then, in Revelation 7, we see that rapture is not going to happen until after the antichrist is revealed and after he unleashes the great tribulation on Christians. This is in line with all the Scriptures we have observed so far. Notice they were only marked out just before the wrath of God was about to be unleashed. They were not sealed/taken while the great tribulation was going on. They were not sealed while the first seals through the sixth seals were being unsealed. Now let us see what happens after the Jewish people that feared God and the Christians from all over the world were shielded; Revelation 8:1–7:

> *1, And when he had opened the seventh seal, there was silence in heaven about the space of half an hour. 2. And I saw the seven angels which stood before God, and to them were given seven trumpets. 3. And another angel came and stood at the altar, having a golden censer; and there was given unto him much incense, that he should offer it with the prayers of all saint. upon the golden altar which was before the throne. 4 And the smoke of the incense, which came with the prayers of the saints, ascended up before God out of the angel's hand. 5. And the angel took the censer, and filled it with fire of the altar, and cast it into the earth and there were voices, and thunderings, and lightnings, and an earthquake. 6. And the seven angel which had the seven trumpets prepared themselves to*

sound. 7. The first angel sounded, and there followed hail and fire mingled with blood, and they were cast upon the earth: and the third part of trees was burnt up, and all green grass was burnt up.

Notice what happens when the first angel sounds. The wrath of God is poured on earth. But thank God those that fear God (both Jewish and Christians) are shielded from the wrath. Notice that God doesn't send any angel to carry out this protection (for the saints) before the first seal is opened. Neither does He do that just before the second, third, fourth or sixth seal. He does that when the wrath of God is about to be poured out, which is the seventh seal that ushers in the seven trumpets.

So far, we have allowed the Bible speak for itself. No Greek meaning of any word, in order to create a narrative that only an individual can understand, has been used. No deeper meaning of any words used has been interpreted. No allegory has been used to create a narrative that doesn't exist. We have just simply pointed out the Scriptures. No magnifying lens has been put on any word in order to show the meaning behind any word. And I believe what has been pointed out is easy to see. You don't need to have the eye of an eagle or the understanding of Methuselah to see it. It is plain for all to see. Rapture **WILL NOT HAPPEN UNTIL AFTER THE GREAT TRIBULATION**. The next question is, can you accept it as a biblical truth?

Chapter 16

The Big Question

Knowing what we know about the great tribulation, the big question is, why would a good God allow those who serve Him faithfully to go through the great tribulation? The issue with most Christians is that they cannot fathom how a good God would be so wicked as to allow His children to go through the most difficult times in the history of humanity. During this period, Christians will be left completely at the mercy of the antichrist, with little or no help from God. They just cannot understand how such a good God would do that to His children. Hence, they'd rather take the stance that the beloved Children of God will be taken by rapture out of the earth so that only those who do not take their walk with God seriously will be left to suffer. Hence, that will make God look good to them. God is not that wicked; He would never allow those who love Him go through the great tribulation is what they say. Let's see whether this is going to hold when we look through the Scriptures for the answer.

Our example

Jesus Christ is the second person in the God head. He came to earth as a human in order to save humanity. When He was about the age of thirty, God introduced Him to His world in a grand style. Look at it here: Matthew 3:16–17:

> *16. And Jesus, when he was baptized, went up straightway out of the water: and, lo, the heavens were opened unto him, and he saw the Spirit of God descending like a dove, and lighting upon him: 17. And lo a voice from heaven, saying, This is my beloved Son, in whom I am well pleased.*

Can you see how heaven introduces Him? God Himself says that Jesus is His beloved Son. If that were where it ends, it would still have meant a lot. But heaven goes further to say God is well pleased with Him. That's remarkable. It is clear to us from this that God loved Jesus very much, yet that did not prevent Jesus from dying a gruesome death on the cross. Look at what happened the night before His crucifixion; Matthew 26:38–39:

> *38. Then saith he unto them, My soul is exceeding sorrowful, even unto death: tarry ye here, and watch with me. 39. And he went a little further, and fell on his face, and prayed, saying, O my Father, if it be possible, let this cup pass from me: nevertheless, not as I will, but as thou wilt.*

This was one of the greatest hours of need for Christ. He would have wanted the Father to let the cup pass over Him if it was possible. But it wasn't possible. He had to go through it to accomplish the Father's will. On the cross, He had to bear the sins of the whole world. God is light, and in Him there is no darkness at all (1 John 1:5). What this means is that God cannot behold sin. God, despite His great love for His only begotten Son, turned His back on Him. Jesus was left to suffer alone. It was the only way. He had to go through the cross and hell to reconcile us back to God. I don't know how God felt when Jesus was going through this very difficult situation, but I believe it would have been unbearable. But that didn't make God stop Him from going through the situation. What Jesus went through was so bad that He was unrecognizable (Isaiah 52:14). This is an example for us. If God could permit Jesus, whom He loved dearly, to go through something that was probably worse than the coming great tribulation for an ultimate purpose, I don't think we can be spared. Someone might say, "Oh no, Jesus had to go through that so we don't have to go through the same." This is a very valid point. But let's consider the lives of other people to see how God dealt with them.

Let's look at some passages to see what the character of God is concerning these kinds of situations; Isaiah 43:1–2:

> *1. But now thus saith the LORD that created thee O Jacob, and he that formed thee, O Israel, Fear not: for I have redeemed thee, I have called thee by thy name; thou art mine. 2. When thou passes through the waters, I will be with thee; and through the rivers, they shall not overflow thee when thou walkest through the fire, thou shalt not be burned; neither shall the flame kindle upon thee.*

216

Notice what God says in the above passages. In verse one of the above, God professes His love for Israel (which includes Christians). Pay attention to the second verse. After telling Israel (and Christians) how much He loves them, He starts telling them how He will demonstrate His love to them. First, He says when we pass through the waters, He will be with us. Isn't that fantastic? Notice what God doesn't say. He doesn't say He will prevent us from going through the waters. He says when you pass through. He doesn't say if we pass through. He says when. What is the difference? "If we pass through" means we might never pass through, while "when we pass through" means it's just a matter of time, we shall pass through the waters. It's the same thing with river, fire, and flame. Notice that the intensity of the situation increases as He progresses. Also notice that in none of the situations does He say He is going to prevent us from going through. It means to me that it is necessary we go through. The only thing He guarantees is that while you are in the difficult situation, He will be with you in it. He doesn't say He will take you out of it. He says He will stay in the situation with you while you continue to go through so that you won't be overwhelmed. Isn't that interesting? Here we see the character of God when it comes to tribulation, persecution, or any difficult time in the life of a Christian.

The Genesis 22 Situation

God demonstrates this character in the lives of all that walk with Him. The purpose may be to achieve different goals in the life of each individual, but the truth remains that all that must walk with God must be able to stand, no matter what confronts them. Look at how Paul puts it in 2 Timothy 3:12:

> *12. Yea, and all that will live godly in Christ Jesus shall suffer persecution.*

Now then, in Genesis 22, the Bible says in Verse 1 that God did tempt Abraham; Genesis 22:1 –2:

> *1. And it came to pass after these things, that God did tempt Abraham, and said unto him, Abraham: and he said, Behold, here I am. 2. And he said, Take now thy son, thine only son Isaac, whom thou lovest, and get thee into the land of Moriah; and offer him there for a burnt offering upon one of the mountains which I will tell thee of.*

Now then, we can see in Verse 2 what is required of Abraham He needs to take his most loved son to a mountain God Himself wil tell him of and offer him as a sacrifice. This is the same son he ha waited twenty-five years to get. You can imagine how much joy thi child would have brought to him. Now the child must be offered as a sacrifice. God specifically mentions the son whom he loves and mentions him by name so he won't pick any other. To cut the very long story short, Abraham obeys without mentioning it to anyone. Not hi wife, not his servants, not even Isaac. Abraham starts his journey to the mountain where he is to offer Isaac. It is a three-day journey from where he lives; Genesis 22:3–4:

> *3. And Abraham rose up early in the morning, and saddled his ass, and took two of his young men with him, and Isaac his son, and clave the wood for the burnt offering, and rose up, and went unto the place of which God had told him. 4. Then on the third day Abraham lifted up his eyes, and saw the place afar off.*

He walks the entire journey without a word from God. One would think that the fact that he takes the three-day journey would have convinced God that he has passed the test. But that is not how God operates. He doesn't prevent us from going through water. He only promises to be in the water with us. God only intervenes when Abraham lifts up his hand, with the knife in it, towards Isaac's neck.

You might say, "Oh no, that does not directly relate to the issue of discussion." Alright, let's consider a more direct matter; Daniel 3:5–6:

> *5. That at what time ye hear the sound of the cornet, flute, harp, sackbut, psaltery, dulcimer, and all kinds of musick, ye fall down and worship the golden image that Nebuchadnezzar the king hath set up: 6. And*

> *whoso falleth not down and worshippeth shall th*
> *same hour be cast into the midst of a burning fier*
> *furnace.*

I am sure a lot of us are familiar with this story. This was a tim in history when most part of the world was ruled by one of the greate empires on earth— the Babylonian. At this time, Nebuchadnezza was the king. He was known to be a very proud man. He set up a image of himself in a public square and commanded everyone unde his reign to bow to the image at the sound of all kinds of music. It almost certain that similar situations will occur during the era of th antichrist as stated in Revelation 13:14–15:

> *14. And deceiveth them that dwell on the earth by th*
> *means of those miracles which he had power to do i*
> *the sight of the beast; saying to them that dwell on th*
> *earth, that they should make an image to the beas*
> *which had the wound by a sword, and did live. 15. An*
> *he had power to give life unto the image of the beas*
> *that the image of the beast should both speak,* ***an***
> ***cause that as many as would not worship the imag***
> ***of the beast should be killed.***

Now then, consider the above passage from Revelation 1 which will occur at the peak of the reign of the antichrist. The proph of the antichrist, who will be the head of the religion (one worl religion) that the antichrist will set up, will build an image of the beas and set it up in a public place for all to see. Every human on earth will be forced to worship the image. Whoever refuses to worship the image will be put to death. Can you see that this is exactly what happened in the days of Nebuchadnezzar? They both set up images of the ruler. They both required the image to be worshipped. They both put a penalty of death on whoever fails to worship the image. This is a very good example to use and it meets all qualifications for the current discussion.

Now then, let's go on with the story in Daniel and see how God dealt with the issue. This will tell us a lot about the nature/character of God concerning the matter we are discussing. Now then, after Nebuchadnezzar set up his image, everyone had no choice than to worship the image. However, three men were caught disobeying the direct orders of the emperor. They refused to bow to the image. Words quickly reached the king concerning these three men. The king decided to give them another opportunity to save their lives. Daniel 3:14:15:

> *14. Nebuchadnezzar spake and said unto them, Is it true, O Shadrach, Meshach, and Abednego, do not ye serve my gods, nor worship the golden image which I have set up? 15. Now if ye be ready that at what time ye hear the sound of the cornet, flute, harp, sackbut, psaltery, and dulcimer, and all kinds of musick, ye fall down and worship the image which I have made; well:*

> *but if ye worship not, ye shall be cast the same hour into the midst of a burning fiery furnace; and who is that God that shall deliver you out of my hands?*

The men refused and responded to the king without an iota of care for their lives in the most profound way: Daniel 3:16–18:

> *16. Shadrach, Meshach, and Abednego, answered and said to the king, O Nebuchadnezzar, we are not careful to answer thee in this matter. 17. If it be so, our God whom we serve is able to deliver us from the burning fiery furnace, and he will deliver us out of thine hand, O king. 18. But if not, be it known unto thee, O king, that we will not serve thy gods, nor worship the golden image which thou hast set up.*

Can you see that? It is clear that they had no fear for their lives. Now then, when should be the best time for God to intervene? The first best time for God to intervene is to prevent them from being seen. They had refused to bow to the image in their private place. In order to avoid them endangering their lives, God should have covered them with His feather so that no one would see them or notice that they didn't bow. After all, their faithfulness was to God not to man. Their faithfulness was a personal matter. At least He saw their faithfulness to Him. But God didn't show up then. The next best time to show up for them was when the king was literally insulted by their response to his second offer. It would have been clear at that point that these guys placed God above all, without caring for their lives. But God didn't show up at that time either. Nebuchadnezzar ordered the fire to be heated seven times more than it was and ordered the strongest men in his army to throw them into the fire. When they were being dragged to the fire, God didn't show up. I cannot tell if they were screaming, struggling, or fidgeting. One thing is clear; they were humans and they were very likely to have had the natural human response to situations like that. They may have said a prayer. They may have said goodbye to their loved ones. Whatever the case, they were not given another chance to redeem their lives. To the fire they went. At the edge of the fire, God didn't show up for them. I believe they themselves would have resigned their faith to death. But God eventually showed up for them. When? Daniel 3:23–24:

> 23. And these three men, Shadrach, Meshach, and Abednego, fell down bound into the midst of the burning fiery furnace. 24. Then Nebuchadnezzar the king was astonied, and rose up in haste, and spake, and said unto his counsellors, Did not we cast three men bound into the midst of the fire? They answered and said unto the king, True, O king.

God only showed up after they were cast into the fire. The God they served is still the same God. He is the same yesterday, today, and forever (Hebrews 13:8). Nebuchadnezzar didn't make Him change;

the antichrist won't make Him change. It is His nature to allow His children to go through fire so that they will come out as pure as gold at the other end. Hence, it is not far from God's nature, if His intention is for us to go through the great tribulation.

We can go on and on citing various examples. What about Daniel and the lion's den? When did God show up? After Daniel was thrown into the den. Not before. The same goes for all the apostles. They all died at the hands of men. Peter was crucified upside down at His request. Paul was beheaded, Thomas was skinned alive in India, John was thrown into a hot boiling pot of oil, Steven was stoned to death, many were imprisoned, and many were fed to animals at the sport arena of Rome in the full glare of the public. They died like nonentities even though they served a great God. Do these guys whom we consider the fathers of our faith, have a different God? Has God suddenly changed after their generation? No. He is the same yesterday, today, and forever. He can never change. Hence, the same God that Paul served faithfully, that permitted him to be beheaded, is the same God we are serving, who also will permit us to go through the great tribulation. So, it is unscriptural for us to think that God is now wicked to subject us to the great tribulation.

If we follow carefully the ministry of Jesus, we can see some profound statements He made concerning tribulation or persecution. Let's consider some of His sayings and see whether Jesus is exactly like His Father; Mathew 10:22:

22. And ye shall be hated of all men for my name's sake: but he that endureth to the end shall be saved.

Notice what Jesus says in the above passage. While you are going through hard times, which are brought upon you solely because you are a follower of Christ, if you fail before getting to the end, you can't be saved. Can you see the consistency of this with the nature of God? Let's look at another passage: Matthew 10:38–39:

38. And he that taketh not his cross, and followeth after me, is not worthy of me. 39. He that findeth his life shall lose it: and he that loseth his life for my sake shall find it.

See how Jesus sounds in that passage. More like this race is not for the weak. If you must follow Me, you must be ready to pay the price of following Me. That price involves you losing your life. Can you see that? Someone might say what He means is not literally losing one's life. It just means one has to make sacrifices. Alright, that might be right, but let's see another example: Matthew 24:9:

9. Then shall they deliver you up to be afflicted, and shall kill you: and ye shall be hated of all nations for my name's sake.

The intensity of what you have to go through to follow Jesus seems to be increasing. Notice what Jesus says in the above passage. He says those who will sincerely follow Jesus will be killed. They all shall be hated by people all over the world. Imagine that. Let's look at another passage: John 16:33:

> *33. These things I have spoken unto you, that in me ye might have peace. In the world ye shall have tribulation: but be of good cheer; I have overcome the world.*

Notice the use of language in this passage. In Jesus we have peace, but as long as we live in the world, we shall have tribulation. Notice what follows. He doesn't say He will do anything to stop us from going through it, neither does He say we won't go through it. He says, cheer up, I have overcome the world. What does that mean? It is a statement of consolation. Telling us that no matter the level of tribulation brought upon us by the world, we can easily go through it without being broken because the world has already been defeated.

We can examine Scripture upon Scripture, we will still find that the tone is exactly the same. God will never prevent us from going through a situation. He will always be with us in the situation while we go through it. Jesus has warned us in several ways that we must, as a necessity, go through difficult situations by virtue of the fact that we decided to follow Him. Hence, it is completely against the general tone of the Bible for someone to suggest that we shall be raptured out of the great tribulation. The early apostles seemed to understand this tone perfectly. Let's look at one or two passages about that: Romans 12:12:

> *12. Rejoicing in hope; patient in tribulation; continuing instant in prayer;*

Notice what the Apostle Paul is saying in this passage. He is trying to give advice regarding the right action in certain situations. He gives three situations a Christian can find his/herself in and what to do in the same. Look at the second situation: tribulation. What do you do when in tribulation? Have patience. He knows that patience is a must for us to go through tribulation. What he now wants us to know is how to behave while going through tribulation. Patience is the right attitude while in tribulation. Why patience? Because you have to go through without expecting any way out. Now then, let's turn to another apostle to learn more about why patience is the most important virtue while in tribulation; James 1:2–4:

> *2. My brethren, count it all joy when ye fall into divers temptations; 3. Knowing this, that the trying of your faith worketh patience. 4. But let patience have her perfect work, that ye may be perfect and entire, wanting nothing.*

Can you see that? Tribulations come to try our faith. Why does our faith need to be tried? So that we can be perfect and fully developed and lacking in nothing. Someone may say, "Oh yes, it is expected to go through tribulation as Christians, but we won't go through the great tribulation." I have a simple question to ask before we look fully into that. If what we call "normal" tribulation has the ability in it to make us perfect, what will the great tribulation do? Have you noticed that Christ is only coming for a perfect church? Do you think the church as it is today is perfect enough to be the bride of Christ? What other tribulation can bring the level of perfection required for the church other than the great tribulation?

What does God hope to achieve in the Church with the great tribulation?

This is another question we should attempt to answer before concluding this issue. This means that we have to do a little examination on why Christians must go through the great tribulation. I believe that as far as Christianity is concerned, nothing happens to us by chance. Every experience we have and will have is a cumulative of what God permits in our lives to bring us to perfection. Remember what God says in Jeremiah 29:11:

> *11. For I know the thoughts that I think toward you, saith the LORD, thoughts of peace, and not of evil, to give you an expected end.*

228

What matters to God is for us to reach that expected end He has determined for us. So, He will permit and allow and bring and do whatever it takes for us to become who He wants us to be. Now then, there are times we choose not to go His own way. We make wrong choices, which have dangerous consequences. That is not a tribulation or trial of your faith, just like Peter puts it in 1 Peter 2:20A:

> *20. For what glory is it, if, when ye be buffeted for your faults, ye shall take it patiently? but if, when ye do well, and suffer for it, ye take it patiently, this is acceptable with God*

You see that? The consequences of your errors are not part of the journey God is taking us through. They are not part of what God permits in order to bring us to an expected end. They are the suffering brought upon us by our foolishness and by choosing to go our own ways. They sometimes even delay or distract us from the track God has planned for us. There are some mistakes that might even be irreparable. However, our God is gracious. There is no story in any human life that heaven cannot rewrite, if such is brought before God wholeheartedly.

Now then, back to the great tribulation: God has designed it for a specific purpose. One of the major purposes it has been designed for is to make the church, which is the bride of God's beloved Son, to be as perfect as His Son, Jesus. Look at what heaven expects the bride to be; Ephesians 5:27:

27. That he might present it to himself a glorious church, not having spot, or wrinkle, or any such thing; but that it should be holy and without blemish.

Can you see that? The church must not have any spot or wrinkle or anything that defiles. The church must be holy and without blemish. It is clear that the current church does not fit this description. There might be individuals scattered all over different parts of the world and in different assemblies who fit these criteria, but the church of God on earth as a whole still has a very long way to go. The greater percentage of the current church sees Christianity as a means to make life easy. Our current popular slogan is give me, give me, give me. You rarely see anyone who says, Lord make me. All of us come to church to have our needs met. That version of Christianity can get the church nowhere in this dispensation. How else can God bring out pure gold from this unrefined treasure other than to subject it through heat Notice that the heat that purifies gold is not intended to destroy the gold. It is intended to destroy the impurity. God wants to get the church to the purest state the church has ever known. The only way to achieve that is to pass the church through a process it has never passed through before. Look at how Daniel puts it in Daniel 11:35:

35. And some of them of understanding shall fall, to tr_ them, and to purge, and to make them white, even t_ the time of the end: because it is yet for a tim_ appointed.

Notice how it is put in this passage. Those with understanding shall fall. Why shall they fall? They shall fall in order to try them. Let's take a pause here to consider the words: to try. The words *to try* are gotten from a Hebrew word, **tsaraph,** which means to fuse a metal, that is to refine or melt (for the purpose of taking out impurities from the metal) and make it pure, to purge away. Can you see that? That is amazing. The last person that wants this to happen to the church is the devil. Hence, he will do everything possible to make sure we are unprepared to go through the heat. Remember the first warning of Jesus concerning this matter: Let no man deceive you. Now then, notice that the purpose for them to be tried is also stated in the passage. It says, "to make them white." Can you see that? Who wants the church to be white, holy, without any spot, wrinkle, or blemish? God. Why? Because He wants the best for His Son. God will accept nothing less.

Now then, what does God need to do to bring the church to the state He wants the church to be in? Look at what He is going to do as prophesied by Daniel in Daniel 7:25:

> *25. And he shall speak great words against the most High, and shall wear out the saints of the most High, and think to change times and laws: **and they shall be given into his hand** until a time and times and the dividing of time*

231

Notice the bolded phrase. It says the saints shall be given into his hand. Who else can give the saints to the antichrist to try? Remember what happened to Job? God lowered the edge around Job and gave the devil an opportunity to try Job. The same phrase can be used for Job. And Job was given into his hand for about nine months. Can you see the similarities? Job 1:11–12:

> *11. But put forth thine hand now, and touch all that he hath, and he will curse thee to thy face. 12. And the* **LORD said unto Satan, Behold, all that he hath is in thy power; only upon himself put not forth thine hand.** *So Satan went forth from the presence of the LORD.*

Can you see that? At the end of the trial, Job receives a double portion of the anointing he has had before the trial. In the same way the church will come out of the trial purer.

Now then, going back to Daniel, notice the phrase used in the particular verse about what the antichrist will do to the saints? He will wear them out. The words "wear out" are derived from a Hebrew word that means to afflict. The saints will be given to him (the antichrist, and in extension, the devil) to afflict them. Look at how John reports the same situation in Revelation 13:7

> *7 And it was given unto him to make war with the*

saints, *and to overcome them: and power was given him over all kindreds, and tongues, and nations.*

Can you see that? To make war with the saints and to overcome them. Also notice that permission is given unto him the same way permission was given to Satan over Job and the same way permission was given to the power of darkness over Jesus. See what Jesus says about that in Luke 22:52–53:

> *52. Then Jesus said unto the chief priests, and captains of the temple, and the elders, which were come to him, Be ye come out, as against a thief, with swords and staves? 53. When I was daily with you in the temple, ye stretched forth no hands against me: but this is your hour, and the power of darkness.*

Did you notice what Jesus says in these verses? It is the hour of darkness. Meaning Jesus was committed to them for a while for a purpose. Look at another way Jesus puts the same event in Mark 9:31:

> *31. For he taught his disciples, and said unto them, The Son of man is delivered into the hands of men, and they shall kill him; and after that he is killed, he shall rise the third day.*

Here, Jesus is preparing the mind of His disciples on what is to come so they won't be caught unawares. Notice what He says to them. The Son of man will be delivered into the hands of men. Tribulation seems to be a good tool to bring out the best in Christians. We have seen that in different characters of the Bible. If "regular" tribulation is capable of making a Christian come out as gold, what will the great tribulation do? To say that the church will not be around during the great tribulation is to deprive Christ of the perfect bride that is due Him. The only person that can create that kind of doctrine is the devil.

Now then, the Bible gives us a glimpse of some of the things the Christians will suffer at the hands of the antichrist. Let's consider some of them; Daniel 11:33:

> *33. And they that understand among the people shall instruct many: yet they shall fall by the sword, and by flame, by captivity, and by spoil, many days.*

They will be killed by sword and by flame. Some will be imprisoned. Look at what happens when the fifth seal is opened; Revelation 6:9–11:

> *9. And when he had opened the fifth seal, I saw under the altar the souls of them that were slain for the word of God, and for the testimony which they held: 10. And they cried with a loud voice, saying, How long, O Lord, holy and true, dost thou not*

*judge and avenge our blood on them that dwell on
the earth? 11. And white robes were given unto
every one of them; and it was said unto them, that
they should rest yet for a little*

Notice what John sees when the seal is opened. He sees souls
of Christians who were killed by the antichrist. Now then, why are the
Christians subjected to death? John gives us a hint in Revelation
12:11;

*11. And they overcame him by the blood of the Lamb,
and by the word of their testimony; and they loved not
their lives unto the death.*

Notice how they overcome the antichrist. By the blood of the
Lamb and by the words of their testimonies. While they are doing that,
their lives will be endangered. But that will not deter them from
continuing. Hence, the more the enemy kills them, the more
victorious they are. Our victory is in the killing. The enemy killed
Jesus on the cross and thought that was the end of it all. He didn't know
that the death on the cross was a great victory for all for the rest of
eternity. Look at how Paul puts it in 1 Corinthians 2:7–8:

*7. But we speak the wisdom of God in a mystery, even
the hidden wisdom, which God ordained before the
world unto our glory: 8. Which none of the princes of*

this world knew: for had they known it, they would not have crucified the Lord of glory.

Notice what Paul says in the above passage. They crucified the Lord of glory because they didn't know the wisdom of God. They did not know that God sowed Jesus as a seed. A seed must first die before germinating. Now we have many Jesuses scattered all over the world reproducing the works of our Lord who was only located in Jerusalem. That is the power of the wisdom of God, which the world can never know. Again, God is about to do the same thing with the many little Jesuses scattered all over the world. But unfortunately, a greater percentage of the church today see no wisdom in Christians facing the great tribulation. Look at how Isaiah compares the way we think with the way God thinks; Isaiah 55:8–9:

> *8. For my thoughts are not your thoughts, neither are your ways my ways, saith the LORD. 9. For as the heavens are higher than the earth, so are my ways higher than your ways, and my thoughts than your thoughts.*

His ways are always higher than our ways. I remember the story of the young man that went to evangelize in a town. Every single person in that town served a particular idol, and they were highly intolerant of Christianity. After the third day of evangelizing, the people of the town caught him and cut off his head. They separated his head from his body and put it by the entrance of the town with an inscription to warn other Christians from coming to the town. Many may say, "How can God make such a thing happen to someone who served Him faithfully?" That's the human point of view. God's way is far from ours. Today, over 30 percent of the population of that town are Christians. We don't know the exact population of the town. But let us assume there are one million people in the town. This means there are over three hundred thousand Christians in the town. One seed sown brought about thousands. That's what we know for now. Those thousands will turn into millions in the future. Now then, do you know the miracle in the story? The young man lives on. How amazing is our God.

Now then, what is the purpose of the Church going through the great tribulation? I believe there are many purposes God has in mind to do anything because the ways of God are past finding. But John tells of one clear purpose in Revelation 19:7–8:

> 7. *Let us be glad and rejoice, and give honour to him: for the marriage of the Lamb is come, and his wife hath made herself ready. 8. And to her was granted that she should be arrayed in fine linen, clean and white: for the fine linen is the righteousness of saints.*

Can you see the above passage? The church has made herself ready. How? By going through the great tribulation without forsaking

Christ. They sacrificed their lives for what they believed. Hence, they were qualified to wear that clean and white gown. Is this unique to the current believers? No. We have great company who died gruesome deaths for their faith. Many were fed to lions; many were burnt to death for refusing to forsake Jesus. Many were crucified with fire underneath. Someone like Thomas was skinned alive. Can you imagine that? I don't know how the great tribulation will be, but I don't think it will be far beyond what these early disciples went through. Imagine putting someone in boiling oil. They did that to John. The disciples didn't ask God any questions. They didn't think it wicked to go through such an ordeal. In fact, the Bible records that they counted it all as joy to be partakers in God's kingdom. Look at how it is put in Acts 5:41:

> _41. And they departed from the presence of the council, rejoicing that they were counted worthy to suffer shame for his name._

Can you see that? They were the first leg of the race. They gladly enjoyed suffering in the name of Christ. We are the last leg and the most important part of the race, yet we are afraid of suffering for Christ. Many are diligently waiting for rapture to take them away from what is coming. May God help us.

The Second Coming and Rapture

Before we conclude this matter, lets address the phrase used by many to differentiate between rapture and the second coming. This is also the same phrase they hold onto to support the pre-tribulation rapture doctrine. It is said that there will be seven years in between rapture and the second coming. The doctrine goes further to say that rapture is when Christ comes **for** His church and the second coming is when Christ comes **with** His church. According to the doctrine, when Christ comes for His church, only the church will see Him. The world will not see Him. When He comes with His church every eye shall see Him, and that is when the wrath of God will be unleashed on earth. Humanly speaking, this sounds very convincing. The only problem with it is that it is nowhere written in the Bible. And that is a really very serious problem, considering the weight of the matter. The next question is, what is the source of this phrase? It seems to me that it is part of the human fabrications about rapture. Briefly, let's consider the position of the Bible concerning the two events: rapture and the second coming. First, let's start with Brother Paul's writing in 1 Thessalonians 4:16–17:

> *16. For the Lord himself shall descend from heaven with a shout, with the voice of the archangel, and with the trump of God: and the dead in Christ shall rise first: 17. Then we which are alive and remain shall be caught up together with them in the clouds, to meet the*

Lord in the air: and so shall we ever be with the Lord.

So far, we have established the fact that the above passage is talking about rapture. Now then, notice how Paul puts the Verse 17. We shall be caught up together with them in the clouds. Who is them? The dead in Christ. We shall be caught up with them in the clouds to meet the Lord in the air. Notice that the passage doesn't say that we are going to heaven. It says we shall ever be with the Lord. What does this mean? It simply means that wherever the Lord is, there we shall be. Now then, let's get some add-ons to this story by looking at what other passages say: Matthew 24:29–31:

> *29. Immediately after the tribulation of those days shall the sun be darkened, and the moon shall not give her light, and the stars shall fall from heaven, and the powers of the heavens shall be shaken: 30. And there shall appear the sign of the Son of man in heaven: and then shall all the tribes of the earth mourn, and they shall see the Son of man coming in the clouds of heaven with power and great glory. 31. And he shall send his angels with a great sound of a trumpet, and they shall gather together his elect from the four winds, from one end of heaven to the other.*

Notice again how it is put in this passage. First, after the great tribulation, Jesus will appear in the sky. Notice what the passage says after the appearance of Jesus. All the tribes of the earth shall see Him. This automatically nullifies the above doctrine, which says at rapture only Christians shall see Him. Notice that just before rapture, the above passage says clearly that all eyes shall see Him. After that, He will send His angels to pick out His elect. Now then, notice the signs talked about in Verse 29. Can you identify that verse from the other passages we have considered earlier? That is the sign that will precede the wrath of God. Let's look at how John the revelator describes the same event in Revelation 6:13–14:

> *13. And the stars of heaven fell unto the earth, even as a fig tree casteth her untimely figs, when she is shaken of a mighty wind. 14. And the heaven departed as a scroll when it is rolled together; and every mountain and island were moved out of their places.*

Notice that these signs precede the day of the Lord. And we know, from what we have considered so far, that the day of the Lord is when God unleashes His wrath on the unrepentant sinners. Notice also, from what we considered earlier, that just before the wrath of God was unleashed on the earth, the people of God were sealed and a multitude of people were seen before the throne wearing white robes. Look at it in the following verses of Revelation 7:9,13,14:

> *9. After this I beheld, and, lo, a great multitude, which no man could number, of all nations, and kindreds, and*

> *people, and tongues, stood before the throne, and before the Lamb, clothed with white robes, and palms in their hands. 13. And one of the elders answered, saying unto me, What are these which are arrayed in white robes? and whence came they? 14. And I said unto him, Sir, thou knowest. And he said to me, These are they which came out of great tribulation, and have washed their robes, and made them white in the blood of the Lamb.*

Notice that just before the wrath is poured out in Chapter 8 of Revelation, and just after the signs of the day of the Lord appear on earth in Chapter 6 of the book of Revelation, Verses 9–14 of Chapter 7 occur. This is in line with what Jesus says in Matthew 24 29–31. Immediately after the tribulation of those days, the time comes for God to unleash His wrath on the earth.

Let's consider another passage to seal it up; 2 Peter 3:10:

> *10. But the **day of the Lord** will come as a thief in the night; in the which the heavens shall pass away with a great noise, and the elements shall melt with fervent heat, the earth also and the works that are therein shall be burned up.*

Notice how that passage starts. It clearly calls the day, the day of the Lord. This has left us without a doubt that the sign we see in Verse 29 of Matthew 24 is talking about the day of the Lord.

Going back to Matthew 24:29, we can see that Jesus doesn't separate the two events—rapture and the second coming—as two different days, neither does He insinuate that they are seven years apart. From what we saw in Matthew, Jesus puts the two events on the same day. Let us look at it again; Matthew 24:29–31:

> *29. Immediately after the tribulation of those days shall the sun be darkened, and the moon shall not give her light, and the stars shall fall from heaven, and the powers of the heavens shall be shaken: 30. And then shall appear the sign of the Son of man in heaven: and then shall all the tribes of the earth mourn, and they shall see the Son of man coming in the clouds of heaven with power and great glory. 31. And he shall send his angels with a great sound of a trumpet, and they shall gather together his elect from the four winds, from one end of heaven to the other.*

If we are to narrate the above passage sequentially using only the parts relevant to the current subject of discussion, it will sound like this: Immediately after the great tribulation, the elements will begin to give signs to show that the day of the Lord is here, and then, after the wrath of the Lord has been accomplished, Jesus shall appear in the sky at the second coming and the eyes of everyone on earth shall see Him coming in the sky. Then He will send His angels with a great sounding of a trumpet to gather His elect from the four corners of the earth. You will notice that I haven't added anything that is not written in the above passage to the narrative.

Now then, let's consider another passage for more clarification; 2 Thessalonians 2:1–3:

> *1. Now we beseech you, brethren, by the coming of our Lord Jesus Christ, and by our gathering together unto him, 2. That ye be not soon shaken in mind, or be troubled, neither by spirit, nor by word, nor by letter as from us, as that the day of Christ is at hand. 3. Let no man deceive you by any means: for that day shall not come, except there come a falling away first, and that man of sin be revealed, the son of perdition;*

Notice that in Verse 1 of the above passage, Paul talks about two major events—the coming of the Lord and rapture. He says, " . . by the coming of the Lord and by our gathering together unto Him." He can't be talking about the same event. They are two different events joined with the conjunction word "and." Did you notice that in Verse of the above passage? Now then, notice what he says in Verse 3. He says for that day shall not come. He doesn't say "days." It is on a single day that two major events will occur. What are those events? They are the second coming of our Lord and rapture. Again, it is clear from this passage that the second coming and rapture are not separated by years or even days. They both occur on the same day. This also agrees with what Jesus says in Matthew 24 and what John says in Revelation 6, 7, and 8.

Now then, let's take one more passage: 1 Thessalonians 5:1–4:

> *1. But of the times and the seasons, brethren, ye have no need that I write unto you. 2. For yourselves know perfectly that the day of the Lord so cometh as a thief in the night. 3. For when they shall say, Peace and safety; then sudden destruction cometh upon them, as travail upon a woman with child; and they shall not escape. 4. But ye, brethren, are not in darkness, that that day should overtake you as a thief.*

Now then, the above passage looks at it from another angle. Let's look at it together. Notice what Paul says in Verse 2. He sounds like he has told them a lot about the day of the Lord in the past. In Verse 2, he starts by saying the Thessalonian Christians know PERFECTLY that the day of the Lord comes as a thief in the night. You see that? Now then, he goes on further to say that that day of the Lord will come as a surprise to the unbelievers, and none of them shall escape. Notice what he says in Verse 4. But for us believers, that day shall not overtake us by surprise. Which day is that? The day of the

245

Lord. You see that? We can make a few statements accurately from the above passage. It means the believers will still be here when the day of the Lord comes. This also agrees with the other passages we have looked at so far. It also means that although we shall be here when the day of the Lord will bring destruction on earth, we shall not partake in the destruction.

We can take Scripture upon Scripture; they will all point to the same bottom-line: there is only one second coming. And that second coming comes after the day of the Lord, the day in which God starts to unleash His wrath upon the sinners. If we say Jesus will come at rapture, and only believers will see Him, and after seven years He will come again and the whole world will see Him, then we are either saying there is a second and third coming or we are saying there are two second comings. We cannot say Jesus appearing in the sky to take the church is not a second coming and call the next event that is supposedly to happen seven years after, a second coming. If we want to say Jesus coming at rapture is not the second coming, then Jesus doesn't really need to come at rapture. He can as well send His angel to gather His elects without Him coming. Why will He appear in the sky only to go back to heaven to stay for another seven years? There is no other coming other than that. The coming of Jesus at rapture and the second coming are on the same day.

Now then, someone might say, "How then do you explain what Jude said about Enoch?" Let's take a look at it together in the light of other passages that describe the same event Enoch talks about: Jude 1:14-15:

> *14. And Enoch also, the seventh from Adam, prophesied of these, saying, Behold, the Lord cometh with ten thousands of his saints, 15. To execute judgment upon all, and to convince all that are ungodly among them of all their ungodly deeds which they have ungodly committed, and of all their hard speeches which ungodly sinners have spoken against him.*

This is probably where they got the idea of Christ coming with His saint at the second coming. But a closer look at this passage will tell the story a little differently from what the doctrine says and will be exactly what other passages say. Now then, in the above passage, Enoch says the Lord is coming with thousands of saints. What is He coming to do? To execute judgement upon the ungodly. Does that not sound familiar? Let's look at another passage that will explain this further: Daniel 7:21–22:

> *21. I beheld, and the same horn made war with the saints, and prevailed against them; 22. Until the Ancient of days came, and judgment was given to the saints of the most High; and the time came that the saints possessed the kingdom.*

247

Notice how that passage puts it. It looks at it from another angle. Now then, notice Verse 21 of the above passage. Daniel beholds the same horn making war with the saints. Who is this horn? It is the antichrist. The horn (the antichrist) making war with the saints is what Jesus calls the great tribulation. Jesus starts Verse 29 of Matthew 24 by saying immediately after the tribulation of those days and here Daniel starts with the same thing, the horn making war with the saints. Can you see the similarities? Now then, notice how Daniel starts Verse 22. The tribulation continues until Jesus, the Ancient of days comes. And immediately after He comes, judgement is given. Now, going back to what Jude reports about the vision Enoch saw; Jude 1:14–15:

> *14. And Enoch also, the seventh from Adam, prophesied of these, saying, Behold, the Lord cometh with ten thousands of his saints, 15. To execute judgment upon all, and to convince all that are ungodly among them of all their ungodly deeds which they have ungodly committed, and of all their hard speeches which ungodly sinners have spoken against him.*

We can see clearly from the above passage that Enoch picks the same story up from another angle. The angle Enoch picks it from is where the Ancient of days, Jesus, is coming to execute judgment on earth, while Daniel and Jesus (in Matthew) start the story from the past where the antichrist unleashes the great tribulation on the saints, and Jesus and Daniel end the story with a happy ending by saying the saints are delivered from the terror of the antichrist. Jesus concludes it by saying the means through which the saints will be delivered—rapture.

Now, you can see the bigger picture when you combine all the passages we have employed in this section. And it is clear that the second coming and rapture are not events separated by days or years. The events will happen on the same day. Again, we can see beyond all reasonable doubt that there is nothing like Christ coming for the church on a separate day and Christ coming with His church on another day. Look at this compilation:

> *Dan 7:22. I beheld, and the same horn made war with the saints, and prevailed against them. 2 Pet 3:10. But the day of the Lord will come as a thief in the night; in the which the heavens shall pass away with a great noise, and the elements shall melt with fervent heat, the earth also and the works that are therein shall be burned up. Mat 24:29. Immediately after the tribulation of those days shall the sun be darkened, and the moon shall not give her light, and the stars shall fall from heaven, and the powers of the heavens shall be shaken. Rev 6:13–14. And the stars of heaven fell unto the earth, even as a fig tree casteth her*

untimely figs, when she is shaken of a mighty wind. And the heaven departed as a scroll when it is rolled together; and every mountain and island were moved out of their places. Rev 7:1–2. And I saw another angel ascending from the east, having the seal of the living God: and he cried with a loud voice to the four angels, to whom it was given to hurt the earth and the sea, Saying, Hurt not the earth, neither the sea, nor the trees, till we have sealed the servants of our God in their foreheads. Rev 11:15–18: And the seventh angel sounded; and there were great voices in heaven, saying, The kingdoms of this world are become the kingdoms of our Lord, and of his Christ; and he shall reign for ever and ever. And the four and twenty elders which sat before God on their seats, fell upon their faces, and worshipped God, Saying, We give thee thanks, O Lord God Almighty, which art, and wast, and art to come; because thou hast taken to thee thy great power, and hast reigned. And the nations were angry, and thy wrath is come, and the time of the dead, that they should be judged, and that thou shouldest give reward unto thy servants the prophets, and to the saints, and them that fear thy name, small and great; and shouldest destroy them which destroy the earth. Mat 24:30. And then shall appear the sign of the Son of man in heaven: and then shall all the tribes of the earth mourn, and they shall see the Son of man coming in the clouds of heaven with power and great glory. Mat 24:31. And he shall send his angels with a great sound of a trumpet, and they shall gather together his elect from the four winds, from one end of heaven to the other. 1 Thes 4:16–17. For the Lord himself shall descend from heaven with a shout, with the voice of the archangel, and with the trump of God: and the dead in Christ shall rise first: Then we which are alive and remain shall be caught up together with them in the clouds, to meet the Lord in the air: and so shall we ever be with the Lord. Jude 1:14–15. And Enoch also, the seventh from Adam, prophesied of these, saying, Behold, the Lord cometh with ten thousands of his saints, To execute judgment upon all, and to convince all that are ungodly among them of all their ungodly deeds which they have ungodly committed, and of all their hard speeches which ungodly sinners have spoken against him. Dan 7:22. Until the Ancient of days came, and judgment was given to the saints of the most High; and the time came that the saints possessed the kingdom.

Notice that the above compilation can pass for one book. Although there are several other passages we can put in there to make a fully comprehensive story, this is a summary of the event as the Bible puts it. Can you see clearly the sequence of event from above? It starts with the great tribulation. Then, while the great tribulation is going on, suddenly, there shall be signs in the firmaments to show that the day of the Lord is here. But just before the wrath prepared is unleashed on earth, God will ensure His servants are sealed and rounded up. Then after the wrath is poured out, Jesus will start descending from heaven to earth, with great angels with a trumpet ready to sound at the command of the Lord, in physical form that all eyes on earth will be able see. Then, suddenly, after the Lord issues the command for the angels to sound the trumpet and to shout with a great shout, the believers, both dead and alive will be forcefully caught up to meet with the Lord in the sky as He descends to the earth in a phenomenon we call rapture. And together, Jesus and the thousands and thousands of saints come down to earth to execute judgement on the sinners on earth. From this, we can see that the second coming and rapture are two events that will happen on the same day. Jesus coming down from heaven to earth with the arch angel is the second coming while the church meeting Him in the sky as He descends is the rapture. Both events will occur on the same day.

Final Note

It shouldn't be surprising if now we are already witnessing the opening of the seals. Jesus makes a remarkable statement in Matthew 24:8. Look at it:

8. All these are the beginning of sorrows (KJV).

8. All this is but the beginning (the early pains) of the birth pangs (of the intolerable anguish) (AMP).

8. But all these things are the beginning of travail (ASV).

Can you see that? The logical question to ask is what is "all these things?" Or what does Jesus mean when He says "all these things?" We need to look at the verses before Verse 8 in order to know what Jesus is referring to when He says all these things: Matthew 24:6–7:

6. And ye shall hear of wars and rumours of wars: see that ye be not troubled: for all these things must come to pass, but the end is not yet. 7. For nation shall rise against nation, and kingdom against kingdom: and there shall be famines, and pestilences, and earthquakes, in divers places.

Now then, remember the question Jesus is initially asked—What shall be the signs: Matthew 24:3:

*3. And as he sat upon the mount of Olives, the disciples came unto him privately, saying, Tell us, when shall these things be? and **what shall be the sign** of thy coming, and of the end of the world?*

Hence, Jesus gives the signs we MUST look out for to show that we are at the time of His coming and the time of the end of the world. These are the signs Jesus asks us to look for: rumors of war and wars. Someone might say, "Oh no, we have been hearing of war and rumors of wars since the beginning of times." I will say look at what Jesus says after that—the end is not yet. Can you see that? The signs that actually usher in the beginning of the times of the end and the second coming are in the next verse. Nation against nation and kingdom against kingdom. This is not a conventional war. This is a special kind of war. The word nation is from a Greek word—*'ethnos'*—which means race, tribe, and family. Look at what has happened in the world in the last two years. Chants and fights over race. Racism has become a serious bone of contention worldwide. This is part of what Jesus describes as "all these are the beginning of birth pain." Look at another one, pestilences. We have seen one pestilence called COVID-19. It ravaged the world for about two years. Another is coming very soon, which might usher in another round of lockdown for some months. Notice what Jesus says. He doesn't say pestilence; He says pestilences. Now then, another sign Jesus gives is famines. One might say, in this twenty-first century, giving the technology, there will rarely be food scarcity. I will say prepare for one. Ask Sri Lanka and the Netherland and you will see that one is coming very soon. The Netherlands happen to be the second-largest exporter of food and meats in the world, but now they are shutting down their farming system for some strange reasons no one seem to be paying attention to. The next sign is earthquakes in diverse places. As of today, the National earthquake information center of the United States has discovered that there are at least fifty-five earthquakes everyday somewhere on the globe. Can you imagine that?

All the signs that Jesus refers to as the beginning of birth pain are already in our world. What does that tell us? Our generation will see the coming of Christ. Another thing it might be telling us is that we may have already started seeing the opening of the seals. Let's look at it together in the book of the seals: Revelation 6:1–6

> *1.And I saw when the Lamb opened one of the seals, and I heard, as it were the noise of thunder, one of the four beasts saying, Come and see. 2. And I saw, and behold a white horse: and he that sat on him had a bow; and a crown was given unto him: and he went forth conquering, and to conquer. 3. And when he had opened the second seal, I heard the second beast say, Come and see. 4. And there went out another horse that was red: and power was given to him that sat thereon to take peace from the earth, and that they should kill one another: and there was given unto him a great sword. 5. And when he had opened the third seal, I heard the third beast say, Come and see. And I beheld, and lo a black horse; and he that sat on him had a pair of balances in his hand. 6. And I heard a*

voice in the midst of the four beasts say, A measure of wheat for a penny, and three measures of barley for a penny; and see thou hurt not the oil and the wine.

In summarizing the above passages, in these verses we can see exactly what Jesus asks us to look out for as signs of the beginning of sorrows or beginnings of birth pain. In there, you see racial wars, pestilences, and famine. So, I believe we are at the beginning of the end of times. And we shall see the revealing of the antichrist, the great tribulation, and the second coming of our Lord Jesus Christ.

Now then, birth pain usually starts with small intensity and longer duration of contractions. And as the woman gets closer to actual labor, the pain increases in intensity and the duration of the contractions, which cause pain, gets shorter. The world has seen a pandemic that led to a shutdown that lasted almost two months in many parts of the world. It is over two years now, and we have not seen another pandemic other than COVID-19. Definitely, another will come and it will be greater in intensity and shorter in duration before another calamity shows up. We are still going to see famine both of the word of God and of physical food. Beloved, these are dangerous times. We can't sit on mediocrity. Mediocrity is when we are still arguing about the time of rapture. The Bible is clear on the timing. Let us move unto higher grounds. As the devil is preparing for these times so also God is preparing those that want to tune in. You have to pay attention to what heaven is saying to be part of this army. There is whole world of preparation behind the timing of rapture. The moment you open yourself to the timing as the Bible puts it, you have opened yourself to a whole world of preparation that heaven is carrying out, even now, in those who are willing and obedient. Will you join the army of God?

The time of tribulation is a time we will not be allowed to take any form of transportation to travel anywhere because we refuse to take the mark. At this time, in the supposed time of peace, God is already teaching people how to travel without taking the physical form of transportation: traveling around the world in the order of Philip the evangelist. At the time of tribulation, we will not be able to buy and sell, but God is preparing a whole group of scientists who will grow food from the earth very fast, to feed those who are aware of what is coming and preparing for it. Healthy food, not burgers or soda. Has he done it before? Oh yes. He fed over three million people for over forty years without them farming or buying food from neighboring countries. During the great tribulation, we will not be able to have a place to lay our heads since we shall refuse the mark. God is already building sanctuary cities all over the world where His children can stay. That's just to mention but a few things that God is doing to make the time bearable for us.

Another issue we must touch on briefly before rounding off this matter is the issue of knowing when Christ will come. A lot of Christians think we can't know when Jesus will come because Jesus

Himself says no man can know. Look at what Jesus says in the following passages: **Matthew 24:36:**

> *36. But of that day and hour knoweth no man, no, not the angels of heaven, but my Father only.*

Mark 13:32:

> *32. But of that day and that hour knoweth no man, no, not the angels which are in heaven, neither the Son, but the Father.*

Notice what Jesus says in the above two passages. He says no one knows the hour or the day. He doesn't say no one will know the week or the month or the year. Now then, remember that Jesus compares the pain during this period to birth pain. No matter how sophisticated a medical system is, or how experienced a doctor is, they can never know the hour and the day a mother who just got pregnant will go into labor. They can predict the week and month and get it right. But no one can predict the hour or the day from the beginning. That is why doctors put down the normal timing as plus or minus two weeks of the forty weeks of pregnancy. This is the same thing Christ is trying to communicate to us. We shall know the general timing. And in fact, Christ expects us to know. But what we shall not know is the specific timing. Look at how Paul puts it in Thessalonians 5:4–6:

> *4. But ye, brethren, are not in darkness, that that day*

258

should overtake you as a thief. 5. Ye are all the children of light, and the children of the day: we are not of the night, nor of darkness. 6. Therefore let us not sleep, as do others; but let us watch and be sober.

Can you see that? That day should not meet us as a surprise. What does that mean? It means we are expected to know the general timing of the day. We might not know the hour or the day. We just must know the week or the month. Why? Paul gives us the reason. Because we are children of the light. Meaning we should know what the word, which is light, says about the matter. If we know what the word says about the matter, we shall not be caught by surprise. A man whose wife is pregnant knows for sure that after about nine months, the wife will go into labor. Hence, the couple can easily prepare for the arrival of the baby without being caught unawares. However, people outside the family might never know the timing even when the pregnancy starts showing unless they are told. That's exactly what Paul is trying to put across. We know, for sure, the number of years the antichrist will reign for. And we know that after the reign of the antichrist comes rapture. Hence, the moment we see the antichrist on the world stage, we can begin to predict the year rapture will take place. We might not know the hour or the day, but if we put all that the Bible has said about this matter to play, we can predict the month and even the week.

Now then, notice also, from the above passage, that Paul tells us what to do in other not to be in the dark concerning this matter. We need to watch and be sober. Where has he learnt this from? Let's see if we can get a pointer to that. Look at what Jesus says concerning the matter: Matthew 24:42:

> *42. Watch therefore: for ye know not what hour your Lord doth come.*

Can you see that? The same reason Paul is telling us to watch is the same reason Jesus is telling us to watch. They both want us to watch because we can know the general timing if we watch. The only thing we are not expected to know is the specific time.

In conclusion, we shall end on this note of advice Jesus gave to the church; Mark 13:37:

> *37. And what I say unto you I say unto all, Watch.*

Maranatha!!!